A PROPER JOB?

LIVING ON THE RADIO

by Johnny Owen

THIS DAY IN MUSIC BOOKS

www.thisdayinmusic.com

A catalogue record for this book is available from the British Library.

ISBN: 978-1-9162582-9-7

Book design by Gary Bishop

Printed in the UK by IngramSpark

THIS DAY IN MUSIC BOOKS

This Day In Music Books
2B Vantage Park
Washingley Road
Huntingdon
PE29 6SR

www.thisdayinmusic.com

War

The Last Night

The trumpets sound for honour and glory,
But in the conflict the same old story,
The battle is but a death vendor
Yet none of them will ere surrender,
With arrows crossbows echoing round.
Comes the night there is no sound.
The purple sky, a midnight moon,
The starlight drums play a different tune.

Verge of Destruction

You say that you're not a man of war,
But you're building a bomb; what's that for?
Your country wishes to be at the height,
But look at the sky, its nice and bright,
Tomorrow it might not be that way,
Littered with chaos and debris, I'd say.
War causes pain and it causes strife,
It takes away most human life.
Your bomb could drop and leave no sign,
But could take away the world's lifeline.
I know you have a craving for power,
But that craving just might turn sour
If your country too, were wiped away,
So keep your wretched bombs, I say.

John Owen.

My contribution to the school magazine. At 13 years old I was into writing stories. poems and saving the World.

Johnny in the studio during his long running Signal Radio breakfast show

Contents

With love and thanks

Love … To my lovely mum, Marie Victoria, who sadly passed away on the 2nd June 2012. She was, and still is, always there. To my darling wife Lynn for all her love, support and care, which has been totally unstinting. To my son Marc, who has me bursting with pride on an almost daily basis, his beautiful wife Jacqueline and my gorgeous grandson Sean.

Thanks to …

Jon Keighren
Chris Peace
Neil Cossar
John Evington
Andy Jones
Kevin Howard
Lisa Peace
Bill and Penny Mellor
Robbie and Jane and all the HitMix Radio Team
Geoff Lloyd

FOREWORD

Johnny Owen is my best mate. For more than 25 years he has made me laugh, he has made me cry and he's made me feel humble and proud in equal measure. We started working together on the radio in 1992 when I was a budding broadcast journalist in Stockport and he was a maverick presenter, hosting an afternoon show which would become a must-listen across my home town, and further afield. It is remarkable to recall how Johnny would go home every single night after another barnstorming show, and then turn up again the very next day armed with another four hours' worth of fresh new material, all of which could be filed under 'genius'. Some of his big-name rivals on other stations would shamelessly listen to Johnny's show and pinch his best material, passing it off as their own. In the end, Johnny just started calling them out on it and would even announce during his show which the best bits would be for them to use! Going to work in those days was a privilege, an adventure, and we would scramble into the Pineapple pub next door every lunchtime, and spend a fantastic hour unwittingly testing out material for Johnny to take to air that afternoon. The germ of the idea for this book actually started in the Pineapple more than two decades ago, and the biggest surprise is that Johnny has finally got down to writing it, because he can't sit still, hence the nickname which me, Geoff Lloyd and Craig Cash loved to use: 'Jumpin' Johnny Owen!' In the late 90s, our working lives took us all off in different directions, but we've stayed firm friends. Even now, me and Johnny still meet up a few times a year to reminisce about days gone by. And he's always been there with a word of good advice – I always remember on the morning of my wedding to my gorgeous wife Sarah, he said to me: "Try not to cock it up with this one!" Johnny has an ability to tap into a topic and spin it into radio gold, so it's no surprise that his Breakfast Show on Signal Two in Stoke ran for a record-breaking 15 years. His style is unique, and I have never once heard him play any songs back-to-back, he's got far too much to say to allow that to happen. So, what's his secret? Quite simply, enthusiasm. When he starts talking about old TV shows or pop acts that hardly anyone can remember, we are hooked by his mesmeric style which brings his subject matter to life and draws the audience into his world of trivia and nostalgia, creating those 'water-cooler' moments that most presenters simply can't achieve. His warmth and affection for his listeners is surpassed only by his love and enthusiasm for the medium of radio – sitting in a darkened room, playing the songs he's been ordered never to play and talking about things which resonate with an audience of every demographic, from teenagers to grandmothers, from young mums to war veterans, his style is universal. Through a shared love of football, Johnny was there with me when I commentated on an FA Cup final at Wembley, doing the job I love the most, and I can't think of anyone else I would have wanted by my side. When he told me he was ill in 2019, it was a huge shock – Johnny has always been invincible, energetic and anarchic. So, what was his response to being diagnosed with cancer? He came out of retirement and got a weekend job on a radio station called The HitMix in Stafford. He is a machine, powered by the love of his amazing wife Lynn. Thank God he never listened to his dear old mum's advice to 'go and get a proper job' – the world is a much better place thanks to Johnny Owen muckin' about and playing the music.

Jon Keighren Author, Journalist, Broadcaster & Friend

CHAPTER ONE: "Memories are Made of This" Dean Martin, 1956 (Number One)

"What bleedin' planet are you on lad?"
"It's like trying to get through to the man in the bleedin' moon"
"Leslie Welsh is alive and well and living here in Bradford"

Dad loved to invoke the name of Leslie Welsh whenever I'd forgotten to do something. I had no idea what the old man was banging on about, it was only years later I discovered that Leslie Welsh was a music hall memory man, a bit like the character in *The 39 Steps* with Robert Donat who was shot at the end of the film while starring at The London Palladium.

Members of the audience would fire off questions about something that happened years ago, usually sport related and Welsh would give the answer in a flash.

"Who was the referee in the 1948 Cup Final?"
"Mr C.J Barrick of Northampton!"
"Which horse came 3rdd in the 1927 Grand National?"
"Bright's Boy ridden by Jack Anthony."

So, calling me Leslie Welsh was Dads idea of sarcasm. On this occasion I'd completely forgotten to put his bet on at "Old Mrs Pogson's".

Even though betting shops had been legalised a couple of years earlier my dad, like most of the other blokes round our way, preferred to deal with unlicensed bookie Mrs Pogson. For one thing, she gave better odds and there was no tax to pay.

Indeed, the shiny new William Hill betting shop on Ashton New Road stayed largely deserted while "Old Poggy" was usually rushed off her size fours.

There was no subterfuge on my part, I hadn't pocketed the five bob that my dad had left on the mantlepiece together with a note.

5 SHILLING WIN
ELOPE TO GRETNA
2-15 DONCASTER
J. OWEN 7 MOODY ST.

I had just forgotten all about it. After all it was a busy time for me, it was half way through the six-week school summer holiday and there were important football matches to play. I would call for my mates Alan Mason and Jimmy Dinsdale, Johnny Hopkins would appear from nowhere, as would Joey Walton. Billy Mellor would get the 53 bus from nearby

Longsight and before you knew it lads from near and far had turned up hoping to get a game.

I was never quite sure how these matches seemed to arrange themselves. Nobody had phones, nothing was pre-arranged, you just knew that this place was the place to be if you wanted to ruin your new shoes, the ones that your mum had warned you never to kick a ball while wearing them.

My mum would leave the back door open during the school holiday while she went to work at the local box-making company round the corner, Dad meantime would be putting in a gruelling shift as a furnace man for Eva Brothers. That was on the odd occasion that his back wasn't playing up or his rheumatism wasn't giving him some gyp.

I would run home in between games, stick my mouth under the tap. then race out again for another game.

The games usually took place a couple of streets away from Moody Street where I lived, much to the annoyance of the residents who would frequently open the front door of their tiny two-up, two-down terraced house to shout: "Why don't you go and play up your own end?" These appeals were always totally ignored.

The nearest thing we had to mobile phones in those days were homemade "walkie talkies" which were basically two empty cans joined together by a piece of string, so your mum had to come to the doorstep and shout you to come in when it was tea time. All the local women had the uncanny knack of being able to be heard by their child at least half a mile away. They would open the front door, stand on the step and shout your first name … twice. The secret was to higher the pitch on the second syllable of your name. I say secret but all the women seem to have been born with the talent, even if your name had only the one syllable it still seemed to work. My mother's call went like this … jo.....HN ….. jo....HN. At which point you had to announce to your mates that you had to go in for your tea, but you'd see them after. Everybody called my dad Johnny - his family, his mates, his colleagues, everybody - so I was always known as young Johnny, except by my mum who always referred to me as "Are John" in the same way that in Coronation Street Ivy would call her son "Are Brian" and Vera called her lad "Are Terry". My dear mother's favourite oft-repeated sentence in later life when I'd totally disappointed her by becoming a disc jockey would be "Oh, our John, when are you going to get a proper job"

Anyway, it turned out that on this particular day my dad's horse "Elope to Gretna" had come in at 12/1 which meant my dad had missed out on a three quid jackpot. In fairness, that was a small fortune to the old man who, I think, only earned about seven pounds a week doing his job, which was hard, hot, unforgiving toil. I never understood exactly what he did for a living, but he would come home every night looking like his musical hero Al Jolson.

"All I asked him to do was one little job, one bleedin' little job," he continued, looking at my mum while prodding me on the side of the head with his finger. "I tell you Marry, I'll swing for him one day...bleedin' swing for him." Mum's name was spelt Marie, but everybody, including my nan, called her Marry.

My mum pulled me away from my dad who by now was blood red in the face and whispered: "You'd better go upstairs and stay there till your tea's ready." I was more than happy to leg it up the dancers, I can tell you.

Dad always called the stairs the dancers. I came to the conclusion in later years that it was a reference to Fred Astaire the dancer … Fred Astaire … stairs. Get it??

To my dad, that three-pound win would have equated to quite a few pints of his beloved Chester's Mild, at 1/3 a pint in old money, you work it out, I can't.

By all accounts, Dad was the life and soul of his local boozer The Duke Of Edinburgh on the corner of our street, always happy to treat his mates to a few bevvies even if it meant handing over an empty wage packet to my long-suffering mother on a Friday afternoon. Then when he'd left the pub and realised that he was once again skint and he'd be housebound for a few nights he would start shouting and hitting out at both me and my mum. He wasn't a bad man, he could be generous, witty and kind, but too much Chester's Mild and too little money made him foul tempered and vicious and I was scared of him.

We lived at number 7 Moody Street, a name that for some reason always embarrassed me. It was in the run-down east area of Manchester called Bradford. These days I think they call it social housing but then it was just a council house. And barely a house at that. A two-up, two-down slum with a living room, kitchen and two bedrooms. No bathroom … just a cold water tap in the kitchen and a scary spider haven of an outside lav in the back yard next to the coal bunker.

Dad's favourite word by far was "Bleedin" - I never ever heard him use the "F" word but Bleedin' (no 'g') rolled off his tongue with next to no effort.

If Dad was stuck in the house with no money to spend and in a filthy temper, mum would, about twice a week, take me off to the local flea pit, after lying to the old man that we were going to spend the evening at my auntie Ethel's house. If the old man knew my mum had money to waste on a night at the flicks rather than the pub there would have been no living with him.

We would go to the Royal Cinema on the New Road to see Steve Reeves in Hercules or Victor Mature and Hedy Lamarr in Samson and Delilah. Mum definitely had a thing for Victor Mature, I think we saw that film about half a dozen times.

The earliest cinema experience I can remember is going to see Larry Parks as Al Jolson in Jolson Sings Again. When he started singing "Climb upon my knee, Sonny Boy" I burst into tears and ran off into the foyer. I've always been a bit soppy like that.

One night my mum slipped out through the back door while heading for the picture house and I didn't realise she had gone, the sudden realisation that I was all alone with my dad filled me with absolute terror, that is how scared I was of my own father. Which is quite sad, don't you think?

I'm painting a Dickensian picture of doom, gloom and child brutality that isn't quite fair. By and large I had a happy carefree childhood, the good memories far outweigh the bad.

Mum and Dad were a little bit tardy when it came to sending me to school, and when I eventually turned up at Bradford Memorial Junior School I spent one morning in the nursery class, had my one and only ever school dinner, before they realised that I was too old for nursery and should be in the "fives" class. So I was taken to my Nana's house where I was given another "dinner" of beef dripping on toast followed by Ambrosia Rice Pudding then taken back to my new more grown-up class. Memories of Bradford Memorial include warm school milk, which put me off milk for life. The little tuck shop in the corner of the class that sold Breakaway and Bandit chocolate bars at break time as well as Wagon Wheels and Burton's Potato Puffs. No worries about childhood obesity in those days. Also playing "catch a girl, kiss a girl" in the playground, which even at that tender age I found very frustrating because even when I managed to tag my secret love Evelyn Malthouse she refused to entertain the idea of kissing me. Probably because I had no front teeth when I was growing up, my front milk teeth simply did not bother showing up. When I was about eleven four teeth came through at once ... two at the front and two at the back. One day in the playground a lad called Stan offered to demonstrate a Boston Crab on me. Apparently, he had seen it at the wrestling at Belle Vue. Like the naïve little so and so I was, I let him, and it hurt like hell...so we started fighting. One of the teachers, Mr Sixsmith came out and said something along the lines of, if we wanted to fight let's go in the school hall and do it properly. So me and Stan were both reluctantly marched off to the school hall where, surrounded by teachers, we were told we would be having a proper boxing match. The door was firmly closed but we could clearly hear a group of kids chattering outside. The bell went and we squared up, after a few minutes of prodding and poking each other I hit Stan firmly on the chin and he started crying. The round was ended so he could be comforted and while this was going on a girl barged in on the pretext of looking for something or someone and witnessed Stan in floods of tears, she was told to get out and the fight re-started. In those early days you only had to look at me and my nose started bleeding so when Stan brushed his fist against my hooter it opened the floodgates, although I was very brave and, unlike Stan, didn't start crying - the fight was declared a draw. However, by now the female imposter had delivered news of Stan's tears to my class mates and I was carried shoulder high through the streets of Bradford accompanied by much whooping and hollering until we reached my house where dad happened to be on nights and was tucked up in bed. Woken by the kerfuffle he opened the sash window and let rip with a foul tempered volley that sent my adoring fans fleeing the scene. Looking back, I probably had a lucky escape with Stan because sometime later, having been rejected by Marilyn Pilot, of whom you will hear more later, he tried to set fire to the school. Attempting to torch your school was quite popular round our way when I was young, some years later my hated nemesis Anthony Healey, of whom you will hear a lot more of later, tried it at my secondary school.

My early school years were not a great success, not because I was especially thick but because I was painfully shy. One day Mr Sixsmith invited me to stand up and read aloud the alphabet. Now I knew the alphabet from start to finish, had I been in the room by myself there would have been no problem, but having the entire classroom, especially my beloved Evelyn Malthouse staring at me, my mind went completely blank. I desperately wanted the floor to open up and swallow me. As it was, Mr Sixsmith gave out a loud dismissive tut and sent me to the back of the class. For weeks afterwards my so-called mates would shout out in the playground: "So what's after ABC, Owen?"

Speaking of ABC, like a lot of kids my age, my happiest times in those formative years were spent at the local cinema on a Saturday morning at "The ABC Minors Club". A couple of hours of rip-roaring bedlam with hundreds of children a-whooping and a-hollering at the antics of Zorro... the Gay Blade! The rollicking adventures of Hopalong Cassidy! And not forgetting Johnny Weissmuller as Tarzan The Ape Man. In the interval the lady would come around with her tray of Ice Lollies and Ice Cream Tubs complete with tiny wooden spoon and Choc Ices. I think it was a tanner or sixpence to get in and of course we had our own song which we sang with enthusiastic gusto ....

"We are the boys and girls well known as the minors of the ABC

And every Saturday all line up, to see the films we love and shout aloud with glee
We like to laugh and have a sing-song, such a happy crowd are we
We're all pals together, the minors of the ABC.

Happy, simple times.

Me and my mates had a ritual. Before going to the pictures, we would nip to Grey Mare Lane Market and buy some stink bombs off the man on the joke stall. Then it was into the cinema, stroll up to the balcony as if butter wouldn't melt and drop the stink bombs on the poor suckers in the stalls.

Another memory of the ABC Minors club is that it was the scene of my first ever kiss. Or was it? To this day I'm not so sure. Having given up trying to win over Evelyn Malthouse, I began to turn my attention to another pretty young girl in my class. And it was the very same girl who had previously spurned my old sparring partner Stan. Marilyn Pilot was a bit like me in that she was very shy and was never heard saying boo to a goose. Thinking about it...why would you want to? Unlike me she was also very pretty. One day I managed to convince her to let me take her to the Minors Club on the Saturday. Obviously, we met inside because even then I wasn't made of money. In bed that morning I had been practising kissing the pillow and when I was sure my technique was spot on, I was ready to go. It was about time I had my first kiss and Marilyn was the chosen one. As we sat side by side she was engrossed in Zorro's latest predicament while I, for once, had bigger fish to fry. Suddenly there was a lull in the action and I sensed that here was my chance. I slowly put my arm round her, leaned over and went for it … over the top … into battle. To this day I'm genuinely not sure if my lips actually made contact with hers or whether I was still a whisker away, but, with a jolt, she suddenly took her eyes off the screen looked into mine, uttered an ear-piercing scream and ran off. So, my first kiss was either with Marilyn Pilot or Eleanor Rigg a good few years later. We'll hear more of Eleanor later.

My dear mum loved shopping on Grey Mare Lane on a Saturday and in the early days I would go with her. I would mither like hell to go on the roundabout and usually end up driving the open top double-decker bus. This was the days before Asda and Tesco took over the world so when all the household goods had been acquired from the various market stalls, I would be allowed to add to my collection of Dinky Cars off the man on the toy stall, then it was off to the butchers and bakers, etc.

One Saturday, for some reason, my mum forgot to buy my dad's Gillette razor blades, so he reluctantly had to put his jacket on and go himself. Mum was off to the hairdresser's so dad was lumbered with taking me with him. Apparently, he came home two hours later, sat down in his favourite armchair, ordered my mum to put the kettle on then casually said, "No idea where that little bleeders got to. One minute he was there, the next he'd vanished." As I was only about three years old at the time my mum began to have a bit of a fit. She raced back to the market, called at all the shops, asking the same breathless question: "Have you seen our John?" Every time the response was negative. In desperation she legged it round to our local Police Station on nearby Mill Street and there I was, crying my eyes out behind the desk. I did a lot of crying in those early years. By all accounts neighbours and relatives would call my mum a saint for putting up with me. What nobody knew was that I had a medical condition. More of that later as well.

I was never allowed to have a dog although I always wanted one, I was forever coming home with some mongrel stray that I told my mum I'd found wandering the streets, lost and hungry. She would have half agreed to let me keep it when my Dad would come home from work and promptly chuck it out again. We did have an ugly black one-eyed cat that was virtually feral. One day my auntie Angie came to our house with a gold fish she had won on the funfair, along with a gold fish bowl, so we gleefully filled the bowl with water, placed the fish in the bowl and placed the gold fish and bowl on top of the sideboard. We sat on the settee to admire this wonderful creature when the cat appeared from nowhere, scooped the fish out of the bowl and swallowed it before legging it out of the back door chased by my Dad wielding the shovel and cursing. Meanwhile I stayed glued to the settee once again in floods of tears. I had been the owner of a goldfish for less than five minutes.

CHAPTER TWO: "It's a Family Affair" Sly and the Family Stone, 1972 (Number 15)

As far as I knew at the time, my mum had two sisters. In fact, there was a third, Margaret, who I only found out about some years later and of whom we will hear more later. I know, there is a theme developing here.

Mum was the eldest and then there was Ethel. What I remember about Ethel is that she had terrible teeth and suffered from constant toothache. She was also very loud and quite domineering. Nobody messed with "Our Ethel".

The youngest sister by some years was Angie. Now, from what I gathered Angie had been a difficult child who only went to school on the rare occasion that she felt like it and she had a penchant for running away from home and staying away for days, if not weeks on end. When she did come home, more often than not she had a bloke in tow. And the bloke was almost always, as my Nana would put it "a no-good waste of space".

My dad mostly referred to them as "dead legs", a popular nickname for toe-rags and wastrels at the time. One such dead leg was an ex-jailbird who the gullible young Angie had fallen in love with on one of her many excursions, "Little Ronnie", a good-looking young tearaway with a teddy boy hair style and a neat collection of skeleton ties. One Saturday lunchtime Angie and Little Ronnie came round to see my mum. Dad was on the settee with the newspaper over his face sleeping off a very enjoyable session in the Duke of Edinburgh. Mum and Angie decided to take a walk on the market while Ronnie said he was nipping for a pint. I think I must have been playing out at the time. With no intention of nipping for a pint and as soon as the coast was clear, Little Ronnie slipped back in our house through the back door and helped himself to my old man's wallet. Dad and his mates spent that night scouring all the local boozers, but Little Ronnie was long gone. Angie, and indeed the rest of us, would never see him again.

Apart from being reckless and head strong Angie was also generous to a fault, a happy-go-lucky girl, carefree and humorous, and nothing tickled her fancy more than winding up my old man. Now dad was only a very small man, tiny in fact, at just five feet tall. Mum was four inches taller and she was never allowed to wear high heels on their rare nights out together. Back in the day, it was fairly common to see a wife who was taller than her husband, less so today. But my dad was very sensitive about being small, something I found out to my cost at the age of about four or five years old, thanks to Angie and her sense of devilment.

One day she took me to the local grocer's shop run by Mr and Mrs Butterworth, a lovely couple who I remember always had a selection of cakes in the window attracting both the salivating gaze of all the kids in the neighbourhood and any and every passing bluebottle. For some reason Mr and Mrs Butterworth's cake selection was always referred to in our family as 'Fancies', as in "Go and ask Mr Butterworth if you can see his Fancies." On this occasion, the fancy I fancied was a Vanilla Slice. As Auntie Angie walked me home, I had one hand holding on to her hand and with the other I was stuffing bits of Vanilla Slice into my grateful mouth.

Suddenly Auntie Angie stopped, let go of my hand and bent down to speak to me face to face: "Go and ask your dad if he's a midget," she said, before telling me to run the rest of the way home. Well, what happened next can only be described as World War Three played out in our smoky front room. I could not have caused more trouble if I had walked in and chucked a grenade. "Are you a... what do you call it ... erm, a midget, dad?" To be fair dad did try to keep his cool and was fairly slow in coming to the boil. He realised almost straight away that Angie had put me up to it, but the conniving little so-and-so had long since scarpered and left me holding the pin. With my dad threatening to skin me alive, I had no alternative but to run for my life. I ran and ran and ran, tears streaming down my face, not daring to look back. I found myself hiding out in my Nana's outside toilet. Nana and Grandad lived in a house identical to ours but just a few streets away. Meanwhile my mum had gone to my Nana's house to give Angie, who still lived there, a piece of her mind and asked if anybody had seen me. She never thought to check the toilet. I have memories of hiding out in that cold inhospitable lav for hours, sobbing my heart out with only squares of old newspaper hanging on a nail on the back of the door to keep me company. Nobody in our family used actual toilet paper until years later. I was only discovered when my Grandad, Woodbine in one hand, Daily Herald in the other, was taken short. Thankfully by the time I got home Dad had gone to The Swan with Two Necks for a swift gill and my mum made sure I was in bed well before he got back.

Angie may have been a bit of a wild child but like I say, she had a heart of gold and spoiled me rotten. She bought me my first Cowboy hat, which I inexplicably left on the bus on the way home. Not put off by this setback, some years later she also bought me my first Beatle jacket from C&A in Manchester. I loved that jacket, even though it was at least two sizes too big for me.

Auntie Ethel I dare say would have been as generous but the poor woman was always skint. She would frequently send me to the corner shop for one cigarette and one match - try telling that to the kids of today. Everybody in our family smoked like chimneys. Mum and Dad chain smoked Woodbines, Dad especially was never seen without a "woody" between his nicotine-stained fingers. “Get me ten Woodbines and a box of swan,” he would say. “Run there and back and I’ll time you.” Of course I fell for it every time. Maybe that is the reason I have never, ever smoked. I must be one of the few people in Britain, at least of a certain age, who have never had a cigarette in his life.

One day Ethel handed me a lit Park Drive and asked me to hold it while she put some lippy on. I couldn’t bear it and immediately threw the fag on the fire. That was one of the few times I received a belt round the head from Ethel, because I had only just got back from Mr Barrington’s corner shop with one cigarette and one match. Of course, at Ethel’s bequest.

Christmas 1962 and Bradford Memorial Junior School decided to put on a nativity play, and I was given a part. It wasn’t much of a part - in fact, it was only one line, but it was quite important and came right at the start of the play. My mum bought tickets for her and my dad but come the big night my dad cried off with a bad back. A well-worn excuse when he couldn’t be arsed, so Ethel stepped in and took up the ticket.

The school assembly hall was packed with proud excited parents, the lights were dimmed and I waited for my cue. I had to walk from the back of the hall, through the audience carrying a cross and deliver the line. Mr Hines tapped me on the shoulder and I set off. I had just passed my mum and Ethel when it was time for my one and only contribution to the production. “And He Came Down from The Mountain” was as far as I got before Ethel jumped in: “Will you shut your big gob, it’s about to start.”

Let me introduce you to a few of our neighbours in Moody Street and close by. I have to apologise because I am terrible with names so we’ll gloss over that.

Number One was occupied by a father and son, who were both a bit strange. I never saw the father out of the house and the son, who was about the same age as me, never came out to play. Nobody seemed to have any idea what happened to the mother. They were the first people in our street to have a telly, a 12-inch set, black and white, of course, that seemed to light up the tiny room, not that I ever went in the house but me and my pals used to sneak a cheeky look through the window now and again. Watching an episode of Torchy the Battery Boy seems to stick in my mind. The lad must have been deeply depressed and unwell because he was always trying to top himself. He once attempted to hang himself with his dad’s tie but that failed. Then he jumped in the fast-moving Red River in Philips Park, but was merely swept along by the current until he was washed ashore. He finally succeeded when he threw himself off the roof of St Brigit’s church one Friday evening.

Incidentally, when we eventually got our first television set and my Nana came round to see it, her initial observation was that "people look a lot smaller on television than they do at the pictures".

Next door to us at number five lived two sisters who both worked at the nearby UCP Tripe factory. The disgusting smell of the tripe works was the first thing that visitors ever mentioned: "What is that awful smell?" they would say. We, of course were immune to it. The sisters used to bring my dad some free tripe every Thursday wrapped in newspaper. The old feller loved his tripe and onions while me and my mum wouldn't go anywhere near it. I often imagine the board meeting that could have taken place at UCP. The Chairman opens up by saying, "Gentlemen, this is basically a cow's stomach, but we want to try and market it as a cheap but healthy meal. Any ideas what we should call it? Yes, Jones?" "How about Tripe Sir?" "Brilliant, Jones...make a note of that, Miss Peacock."

At number nine lived "Auntie" Mary and "Uncle" Bill. Neither of them were related but I was always told to call them Auntie and Uncle. It seems that back then everybody had an Auntie Mary. Bill used to stand me on his windowsill and whisper: "Go and tell your dad he's a silly old bastard," before chuckling himself senseless. Of course, I would run into our house and say: "Dad, Uncle Harry says you're a silly old bastard." Looking back, I think the words "Uncle Harry says" probably saved me from a clout round the earhole.

An old lady lived alone at number eleven, but her son would visit once a week, usually on a Sunday. He would turn up in his very flash car which, before too long, was surrounded by admiring nippers such as me and my mates. The car was probably a Ford Consul but we took it to be an American Cadillac like the ones seen in Highway Patrol with Broderick Crawford. We also decided that the son must be a gangster who definitely carried a gun. Highway Patrol was the big Sunday night TV show of the day. Crawford played gruff, hard-bitten police chief Dan Mathews, whose catchphrase when signing off on the walkie-talkie was "10-4". At Bradford Memorial on the Monday all us kids would be running round the playground shouting "10-4" even though none of us had any idea what it meant. Crawford would also end every programme by looking straight into the camera and delivering the line "Remember to leave your blood at the Red Cross, not on the highway."

Number 13 on the corner was occupied by a chap who, like most of the men in Bradford, worked at the local pit. He worked regular nights and to supplement his income also served as the local "Knocker-Upper." The Knocker-Upper was a man or woman who would come to your house first thing in the morning and tap on your bedroom window with a big stick in order to wake you up in time for work. This was before the days of radio alarm clocks. Then they would call round, usually on a Saturday morning and collect their sixpence or whatever they charged. My mum always said that I couldn't possibly remember the Knocker-Upper because he retired before I was born, but I would regularly sneak into my mum and dad's bed in the middle of the night if something had spooked me and nod off between the two of them and I can clearly remember the tap-tap-tap on the bedroom window. The question I never got an answer to was: "Who knocked up the Knocker-Upper?"

Just round the corner on Butterworth Street lived the Docherty Family, Mr and Mrs Docherty and the twins Thomas and Michael. The Dochertys may well have been of Irish descent but I really can't remember. At the time, my mum worked at a local box works making wooden crates and boxes, and my Nana would look after me at lunchtime and after school before mum got home from work. When Nana was rushed into hospital with tuberculosis, mum was at a loss as to who was going to "mind" me until Mrs Docherty volunteered. She was a nice woman who, like most of the people in Bradford, struggled to make ends meet, so no doubt she was getting paid to look after me. She had some funny ways did Mrs Docherty. For instance, she would never allow Thomas and Michael to wipe their bottoms after going to the toilet, she thought it was disgusting. As a result, the twins were always digging something hideous from up their short trousers. Anyway, we'll gloss over that and get to the time she served up spaghetti on toast for dinner. Now we are not talking real spaghetti here, in fact this was some years before Panorama had the nation believing that spaghetti grew on trees as part of their famous April Fools gag. No, this was Heinz tinned Spaghetti in tomato sauce, but the thing is, I had never seen anything like it before. I burst into tears and ran out of the house, down the street, across the main road without looking left or right and ran into Queen Street and into the arms of my alarmed mother in the yard of the box works. Gasping for breath and fighting back the tears, I screamed: "Mam, she's giving me worms!!"

Next door to The Docherty's lived the Waterworth's and they were the stuff of legends. Old Mr Waterworth was a tiny man, permanently bent double with back problems. He spent most of the day sitting on the doorstep smoking his pipe and sipping tea out of a mug almost bigger than he was. His wife always seemed to be faffing and fussing round him, looking after his every need. Mrs Waterworth was the spitting image of the great old actress Esme Cannon. If you're of a certain age you might remember Esme played "Brother" Lil in The Rag Trade on telly with Reg Varney and Miriam Karlin, who was much impersonated for her catchphrase "Everybody Out". Miss Cannon also played the old lady in the cafe who was beguiled by Norman Wisdom singing "Don't Laugh at Me" in the film *Trouble in Store*. That lovely old song can still reduce me to tears more than 60 years on:

I'm not good looking
I'm not too smart
I may be foolish, but I've got a heart
I love the flowers, I love the sun
But when I try and love the girls, they laugh at me and run
Don't laugh at me, cause I'm a fool.

It's almost impossible to imagine Mr and Mrs W enjoying nights of passion but they must have had their moments because if our football had popped or gone over the wall, or we were at any kind of loose end, we would pass the time by trying to remember all the people who lived in the Waterworth household. As far as I remember it was 19. 19 people huddled together in that tiny terraced two bedroom house, Mr and Mrs Waterworth and their SEVENTEEN kids. As you can imagine the Waterworth clan tended to stay together and close ranks so we didn't have much to do with the children, but I remember that one of the younger ones was always running away from home. We would cheer as he shinned down the drainpipe at the back of the house before disappearing into the night, only to return a few weeks later with his tail between his legs. However, before too long, he was off again. The eldest son ended up working with my dad at Eva Brothers and dad took him under his wing because he was "a decent lad and a good grafter".

I only ever skipped school once in my life. I'd become pally with a new kid who had come to live round our way who one day persuaded me to "wag it". We spent the day getting up to various kinds of mischief, including stuffing Brillo Pads into our pockets that were on display outside a local hardware store. What did I want with Brillo Pads? Exactly! Anyway, there we were helping ourselves to this poor shopkeeper's livelihood when a woman came from behind, grabbed us both and marched us into the shop. My new friend seemed calm and collected and never said a word while me, in fear of my life if my dad got to hear about it, I pleaded for mercy. "I'm a catholic," I lied, "And I wouldn't normally do anything like this," The shopkeeper gave us a real good talking to and warned us never to set foot in his shop again but thankfully let us go, despite threatening to call the police. That evening my mum came home from work and asked me how I'd got on at school that day, something she rarely, if ever, did. I cleared my throat and readied myself to tell a few porkies when she said: "You liar, you were seen hanging around on the Old Road, wait till your dad gets home!" For the second time that day I found myself pleading for my life and for the second time my prayers were answered. Thankfully dad never did find out, but I worked out for myself that my new "pal" was a bad influence on me and from then on I gave him a wide berth. A couple of years later he was arrested for breaking into houses and trashing them. Most of the lads round our way were little rascals but this lad was a genuine bad 'un and was shunned by the rest of the kids.

CHAPTER THREE: "The Story of My Life" Michael Holliday, 1958 (Number One)

I'm not ashamed to admit that I was a bit of a spoilt kid. Not by my parents, my old man had enough on his plate dealing with Woodbines and Chester's Mild not to mention the bookies. Dad was always skint. Mum would complain that he had been happy to throw his money about in the various hostelries he frequented, but by the time he eventually staggered home, he had spent up and was in a foul, bad-tempered mood because of it. Mum, on the other hand, was very careful with money, not that I ever wanted for anything. If I needed a new pair of shoes, as I frequently did after ignoring her strict orders not to start kicking a ball about, she always found the money from somewhere. We always had decent, if basic, food on the table. If the house needed decorating, she would pay for it or do it herself. I can vividly remember her working round my dad, hanging up wallpaper as he sat glued to the horseracing on the telly, chain smoking his "Woodies" and urging Mum to brew up!

She always somehow found the money to take us away every year for a fortnight at the Robin Hood Caravan Park in Squires Gate near Blackpool. Looking back, the Robin Hood Caravan Park was a grim old place, rows and rows of dilapidated caravans in a field in the middle of nowhere with a "club" a long walk away at the far end next to the showers and the toilets. One time my Dad insisted on entering me for the junior talent show. I really wish I still had the photo of me on stage shaking like a leaf, wearing my cowboy hat and singing Frank Ifield's number one hit "I Remember You".

Nobody in the family could ever comprehend the fact that I became a professional disc jockey, entertaining hundreds of people in a nightclub. Me? Totally unthinkable. Mum would often chide me because if anybody came to the house I would run upstairs to my bedroom to avoid having to speak to them. I wasn't being rude, I really was painfully shy, positively tongue-tied. In truth, I always needed a couple of pints to calm my nerves before getting on stage or indeed behind the DJ booth. In my career, I worked at some of the biggest clubs in Britain packed with a couple of thousand people. I wasn't too bad on these occasions, but if it was a bad night with just a handful of people in the place I would be shaking like a leaf. Strangely, apart from my first ever broadcast on Radio Manchester, I never get nervous on the radio. Sitting in a darkened studio talking to myself has always seemed like the most natural thing in the world.

Dad would bring his mates back to our house after the pub most weekends to continue drinking till the early hours. Mum would be despatched into the kitchen to "sort out the bacon butties" and inevitably, a singsong would ensue. Dad would launch into his full range of the Al Jolson back catalogue, not forgetting a few Nat King Cole classics, and quite often I would be dragged out of bed to join in. I secretly enjoyed giving this drunkenly happy bunch a song or two but was too scared to look them in the eye while I was doing it, so I would crouch down behind the settee before launching into one of the hits of the day. Michael Holiday's "The Story of my Life" was one of my early favourites along with Bobby Darin's "Things": Like a walk in the park (Things) like a kiss in the dark (Things) like a sail-boat ride (yeah-yeah)

If you have ever heard any of my Christmas songs, you'll find this impossible to believe, but in the days before my voice broke I had quite a decent singing voice. Indeed, our music teacher at Bradford Memorial Junior School, a buxom middle-aged woman called Mrs Reid, once said I reminded her of Billy J Kramer (there's one for the teenagers). Anyway, this particular night in Squires Gate I came second to a girl with a talent for tap dancing. My consolation prize was a jigsaw puzzle and I have always hated jigsaw puzzles. Our two-week holiday at the Robin Hood Caravan Park always tied in with the two worst weeks of the year and it seemed to rain non-stop. and our caravan always, absolutely always, leaked. I can vividly remember Mum getting all the saucepans out of the cupboards to place them where they could best catch the dripping water.

Sometimes, if my dad couldn't be bothered coming with us, Angie or Ethel would tag along. Either way we always travelled down in Uncle Bill's car. He was my dad's younger brother and the only one in the family who could drive. Being in a car just once or twice a year meant I always got car sick which necessitated plenty of stops along the way. The cry would always go up "Are we nearly there yet?" to which the answer was usually: "Bloody hell lad, let's get out of the street!"

Apart from Squires Gate and Blackpool, the farthest we ever got was the Belle Vue Amusement Park five or six bus stops away in nearby Gorton. Forget Disneyland, Belle Vue had it all, thrilling heart-stopping roller coasters like The Bobs and The Scenic Railway. They had a zoo where you could actually be photographed sitting on an elephant. You could visit "The Amazing Spider Woman", a mysterious creature, with a woman's head and a spider's body, who had been discovered deep in the African jungle. On a Saturday night, you could watch the famous Belle Vue Aces Speedway team in action. But, most impressive of all, 60 summers and more later, still the most impressive thing I have ever seen in my life, so much so I begged my mum to take me to see it twice: Professor Tomlin's Flea Circus, Fleas on trampolines, duelling fleas, fleas on unicycles. How much fun can you have for 2/6? (that's just over 12p, by the way).

No, it wasn't my parents that spoiled me, it was my Nana and my mum's two sisters, Ethel and Angie, because not only was I an only child at home, I was the only child in the immediate family. Both Ethel and Angie were unable to have kids, so I became a kind of surrogate nipper to both of them.

Years later, I developed a theory about why Ethel and Angie were not able to have children and while I have no proof of this it's not going to stop me from telling you. What initially sparked my suspicion, apart from the lack of children, was when, as a teenager, I just happened to mention to my mum that I had started getting moles on my body. "Oh, they must run in the family," she said "I've got quite a few, and your grandad is covered in them." Aha! Ladies and gentlemen of the jury, I put it to you…

For years, my Nana and Grandad had a lodger, a strange, unfriendly chap who I can't recall ever saying anything, certainly not to me anyway. He spent the entire day in just his vest and trousers studying the racing pages of the newspaper. Now, Grandad frequently worked nights at the Clayton Aniline Company. He was there for over 25 years and I don't think he ever had a day off work in his life. Indeed, he was awarded the statutory Gold Watch on his retirement that he subsequently passed on to me on his death bed. More of that later. It's my theory that while my mum was the legitimate offspring of this reasonably happy marriage, her two sisters were the result of illicit encounters between my Nana, possibly after a few too many Mackeson's, and Roger the silent lodger.

My dear old Nan loved a Mackeson Cream Stout and would frequently send me to the "outdoor" to replenish her stocks. The "outdoor" was always the dingiest room of the local pub, a Godforsaken cold and dark place, where you could wait the best part of a fortnight before somebody noticed you were there. Nan absolutely doted on me but she could be quite sharp with others, usually her long-suffering husband or, as the eldest child, my mum. Apart from Ethel and Angie, there was another sister who died before I was born. Her name was Margaret and she was knocked down and killed by a passing car on the main road outside Butterworth's corner shop while in the care of my mum. Years later, mum told me the story. She and Margaret had spent the day playing on the swings and the see-saw in the park. They bought an ice cream from Mr Granelli's cabin situated just by the park and headed home for tea. This was back in the 40s, Mum was in her teens and Margaret was about six. I often think that Margaret must have been the unluckiest girl in the world, because even in the early 60s, only about two cars a day ever passed down that particular road.

Nan just couldn't help herself. Family get-togethers, say at Christmas, always started well but as the evening wore on and the cream stout took hold, she would start to make off-colour remarks about mum being responsible for Margaret's death. My mum never was one to cause a scene, but I would look at her and see she was getting upset.

Mum was a funny old girl, I can't remember her ever giving me a kiss or a hug or telling me that she loved me, but she showed her affection in other ways. For one thing she was fiercely protective, nobody was allowed to get away with hurting me, either physically or emotionally. One day she sent me to the corner shop. Not Mrs Barrington's shop, because that would have meant me having to cross the main road, but Mrs Cooper's emporium at the other end of the street. I was to come back with two ounces of thinly sliced Prem. If you have never heard of Prem, it was a bit like Spam, only cheaper. It came in a large circular roll and you had to ask the shopkeeper to slice it to your requirements on one of those slicing machines that all the local shops had behind the counter. I entered the shop right behind a woman who said to Mrs Cooper: "This lad can go before me if he doesn't want too much." Mrs Cooper beckoned towards me and said: "Do you want much, John?" I told her I only wanted one thing and moved ahead of the other customer. "Two ounces of thinly-sliced Prem, please," I said. Well, you'd have thought I'd asked for the contents of the entire shop to be wrapped and priced up. Both women gave out a loud exasperated "tut". "Bloody kids," said the customer, followed by another tut. "I see it all the time," agreed Mrs Cooper. "No respect for their elders." I did eventually get the two ounces of thinly sliced Prem, which Mrs Cooper almost flung at me with unconcealed contempt. What I hadn't taken into consideration was the time it takes to haul the slicer onto the counter then re-adjust the settings - about 90 seconds. When I got home, I casually mentioned what had happened and that was it, Mum was off down the street to give Mrs Cooper a piece of her mind.

Although she could be a bit of a wallflower, Mum was never backward when it came to dishing out a clout round the earhole, or a go-a-longer as she called it, as in "Our John, you're not too big to get a go-a-longer." Unlike dad, who flew off the handle at the slightest thing, it took her quite some time to come to the boil, but when she did, you certainly knew about it. I remember one day pushing and pushing my luck until she exploded like a bottle of pop. Unfortunately for me, she had just finished putting coal on the fire and she came at me with the shovel. Eyes bulging and possibly foaming at the mouth, the first two swings of the shovel missed but the third one caught me flush on the temple. I dropped to my knees and actually saw stars. Up until then I thought it was something that only ever happened in cartoons. Had I been walloped by a Joe Frazier uppercut I don't think I could have been in more pain. I was too shocked to cry, but in future if I got a bit lippy with my mum, I made sure the shovel was safely out of harm's way.

On the subject of my mother's temper I'm reminded to tell you about a couple of occasions when I'm sure she might have been tempted to bugger off and leave my dad for a younger, fitter model. Mum was a good-looking woman back in the day, indeed I can remember a school mate coming back to our house and saying: "Blimey Owen, you're mam's gorgeous!"

One day I was waiting outside the box works for her to finish work. I got a bit bored and started swinging on a litterbin that was attached to a lamppost. Suddenly a copper appeared out of nowhere and gave me a proper telling off. Now, I was old school and had been taught to be scared of policemen, so I burst out crying, just as my mum came out of work. Well, she laid into that poor young bobby with a vengeance: "What do you think you're doing? He's not doing any harm, have you got nothing better to do?" It may well have been this particular police officer's first day in the job for all I know, but the poor bloke was left speechless. In the days that followed, that young constable called at our house on a regular basis, always when my dad was out and always on some half-baked pretext. "I'm looking for a dog that's gone missing," or "Have you seen any suspicious strangers lurking in the area". One day, while reading that week's edition of the Dandy in my bedroom, I overheard mum talking to Angie. Apparently, the policeman had broken down in tears, declaring his undying love and asking Mum to run away with him. She told him to stop being stupid and that she was a happily married woman. Happily married? I was never too sure about that.

Then there was Jimmy Mack. A workmate of dad's who used to tag along to all the afterhours piss-ups at our house. He was quite a bit younger than the rest of the blokes and I remember he would sit quietly sipping his bottle of beer while ploughing through a full jar of mixed pickles with one of our forks. Mum did complain to my dad that Jimmy was costing her a fortune in pickled onions. One night, after one of dad's sessions, I was woken up by a noisy commotion coming from downstairs. Dad was storming round the living room in just his vest and undies calling Jimmy all the names under the sun. Apparently, he'd caught them on the settee in the middle of the night deep in conversation, with the pickle man trying to convince my mother to go and live with him. Whether or not there was anything else going on as they shared a settee that night, I really can't say, but dad took a good few weeks to calm down.

It was about this time that I developed a long-running eye infection. Once a week, over several months, my eye would go bloodshot, swell up, then close up. I tended to look a bit like Quasimodo. I ended up missing so much school that eventually the dreaded School Board man came knocking on our door poking his nose in. As I was totally confounding medical science, the decision was made to admit me into The Manchester Royal Eye Hospital, where I stayed for a couple of months. The stay wasn't totally wasted as I ended up winning the under-11s' draughts championship and also the under 11s' twisting competition. As the Twist was a fairly short-lived dance craze, that was probably the last competition of Its type held at the hospital, so I cling to the notion that I am still the holder of that title. Eventually the doctors solved the problem, they discovered a solidified mass of catarrh lodged behind my eye, affecting the eye, ears and throat, so that's why I was always crying like a baby, I wasn't just being a mard arse.

And so, to secondary school.

CHAPTER FOUR: "It's All In The Game" Tommy Edwards, 1958 (Number One)

I wouldn't go as far as to say that I failed my eleven-plus on purpose, but I was pretty chilled about it. My parents had decided that if I passed, I would most likely go to Openshaw High School, which was a bus ride away, but if I failed then it would be Grange Street Secondary Modern just down the road. I had gone past the high school once or twice and noticed they had rugby pitches in the grounds. I had no interest in rugby and certainly no desire to get involved in playing the game, whereas, every time I walked past "Grainey" there would be an enthusiastic game of football taking place in the playground, so when I failed the exam I wasn't too bothered. Grange Street, here I come.

My first form teacher was the gloriously named Miss Fanshawe, an elderly spinster who, rumour had it, was jilted at the altar in her 20s and never recovered. Mind you, since the rumour was started by us kids, there was probably not a grain of truth in it.

I have gone on record as saying that Grange Street Secondary Modern School for Boys was the worst school in the entire country and looking back it probably was. At the time though, it was pretty good fun. The school had no real interest in providing their pupils with a decent education and they had no system in place to take 'O'-levels. You never had to do any homework and there was no school uniform, you could turn up in any old clobber. By and large, I enjoyed my time at Grange Street even though, on reflection, you were guaranteed to leave school with absolutely no qualifications. For a football-mad teenager however it was just about perfect. There was a full-on game in the playground every morning before lessons, which meant wolfing down your Coco Pops before racing to school to make sure you got a game. On Friday lunchtime, there was always a game of Teachers v Pupils, and more often than not, I was chosen to play. But if not, I was pencilled in as the referee, which was a mixed blessing because the school bully Anthony Healey would usually be playing for the pupils and if I gave a decision against him, he would follow me into the outside toilets where we all got changed and unceremoniously beat me up.

It's possibly an understatement to say that while at secondary school football dominated my life. It's really all I ever thought about at the time. It's all down to my Uncle Jack, he took me to my first football match: Manchester City v Blackburn Rovers. I would have been about seven or eight years old and City won the game quite easily, I think it was 4-1. When I got home, I told my dad that I loved football and was now a City fan. I think news that I had joined The Hitler Youth Movement might have gone down better. Dad said that I would support Manchester City over his dead body. "I'll take you to see a proper team next week," he said, and for once, he was as good as his word. For the first and last time in his life, he took me to a football match. Of course, it was at Old Trafford and it ended Manchester United 2 Preston North End 0. Even back in those dark and dismal days it was clear to me that United were a much more glamorous proposition than their sky-blue neighbours. The moment the blonde, slightly balding Charlton glided past the static Preston defence before unleashing a stunning pile driver into the top corner of the net I was hooked, a United fan for life. Denis Law was my real hero and in future weeks I would find myself not really watching the game but watching him. The way he walked, the way he ran, the scrapes he got into with opposing defenders, no wonder they called him 'The King', he was majestic. A few years later, I formed my own football team and called it Denlaw F.C. I wrote to Denis telling him what I'd done and asking for his permission. I was secretly hoping that Denis would offer to buy us a kit or at least a couple of balls, but he never wrote back. For weeks, I rushed to the front door every time a letter came through the post box, but nothing from the great man. I actually met Denis 30 years later and told him about the letter and he swore blind he never received it, but he did say that even if he had got the letter, he wouldn't have sent any money. "After all," he smiled "I am Scottish." Denlaw FC ended up losing just one game all season and we won the league and cup double by a mile.

My time at Grange Street would have been one long happy memory apart from one lad, Anthony Healey. Healey gave me countless sleepless nights, he was a bullying coward, a snivelling sweaty excuse of a human being who picked on me every day for as long as he could and was only stopped when my mother realised what was going on and stepped in, fiercely protective, as I said earlier.

In short, Anthony Healey made my school years absolute hell. He was the biggest, tallest lad in the class, and I was the smallest, so that's all Healey needed to target me. I have no idea what he's doing these days, but I sincerely hope it's life in Strangeways.

Healey apart, life at Grange Street was fun and creative, mainly thanks to my English teacher Mr McMullen who was really into literature and drama. He's the man who got me into the brilliant Just William books by Richmal Crompton, and he loved to put on plays. After a while, he would let me write them along with a creative soul mate called Terence "Tex" Hall. Me and Tex both fancied ourselves as would be playwrights and Mr McMullen would have a quiet word with the woodwork teacher Mr Frost to allow us to skip the hateful woodwork lessons so we could work on our latest masterpiece.

One such masterpiece was a play we wrote about the Secret Service. As you can imagine, this was a subject both of us knew absolutely nothing about, but we reasoned that if we were in the dark, then the rest of the great unwashed at "Grainey" were most assuredly in the same boat. The one and only performance of the production was to take place the day before we broke up for Easter, traditionally a day when no schoolwork was on the agenda anyway. We had rehearsed diligently for, well, at least a week, but felt confident and ready to go. I played an alcoholic spy called Bacchus, as in the Greek God of wine. Little did I know that I would become such a lover of the old falling-down water in later years. The one line I remember saying was "My name's Bacchus and I don't stir without my bottle." The word 'stir' was delivered with a perfect slur, even if I do say so myself. I rather blotted my copybook, however, when half way through the play I was supposed to launch into the song "It's a long way to Tipperary" but at the crucial moment my mind went blank and I could not remember what I was supposed to be singing. There was a pause that seemed to last a lifetime while the rest of the cast just looked at me mouthing who knows what. Then for some inexplicable reason I started singing "Oh when the Reds go marching in, when the Reds go marching in, I want to be in that number." Football again, you see. That, at least, woke up the audience. A few even joined in.

Me and Tex were so wrapped up in writing plays that for a while we would take ourselves off to the theatre so see a professional production. The old man, as you can imagine, was less than impressed. As I was getting ready to go out, he would pipe up with something like, "Hey Shakespeare, don't forget your quill. You might want to make some notes." Then he'd blame it all on my mother: "This is your fault, Marry, for molly-coddling the lad. He's turned into a nancy boy." I'm pleased to say I rose above these comments, turned on my heel and slammed the door behind me.

The one play that sticks in my mind was "Rattle of a Simple Man" about a bloke called Percy who goes to London to watch the Cup final and ends up in a brothel. I embarrassingly dissolved into a fit of nervous laughter when one of the prostitutes stripped off. All a bit too much for a 13-year-old. Incredibly, my mate Tex, also 13 years old, sat through the entire scene straight-faced and totally unmoved, apart from whispering "shut up" every couple of minutes.

I hated woodwork, mainly because I was hopeless. Every week I would totally ruin whatever I was supposed to be working on. At the start of a new lesson, I would look round to see who was absent then go to the store cupboard and find his work from the previous week, rub his name off and replace it with mine. By the end of the lesson, the new piece of work was in tatters and I would hide it behind the cupboard and keep my fingers crossed that somebody else would be missing the following week. The only thing I ever took home from the woodwork class was an ashtray stand, which my mum was delighted with, and actually handed over money for, not to me but to the school. That wonky ashtray stand took pride of place in our living room for years. Now that my mother is no longer with us I can at last confess that it really had nothing to do with me and was the collaboration of half a dozen class mates who each missed occasional woodwork lessons.

I say I was hopeless at woodwork, but to be honest I was hopeless at most of the subjects apart from English, mainly because I loved English but had no interest at all in any other subject, especially maths.

The teachers at Grange Street, Mr McMullen apart, were an odd bunch. Mr Hipwell, the religious education teacher, was a borderline psychopath. He always had the blackboard rubber in his hand ready to expertly chuck at your head with pinpoint precision, or he would sneak up behind you and rap you on the knuckles as hard as he could.

Mr Harris, the maths teacher, scared everybody, even the other teachers. He habitually talked out of the side of his mouth, a bit like Humphrey Bogart. One day, all of a sudden he was not there and he was never mentioned again. We later found out that he had come face to face with a former pupil and pulled out a knife. None of us were too surprised.

Mr Allen, the art teacher, was young and trendy and drove a flashy sports car. If Grange Street had been a mixed school, all the girls would have fancied Mr Allen. He was the first man not on the telly who I ever saw wearing a cravat, but he was a hopeless teacher with no interest in art, or at least no interest in passing on his expertise to the likes of us. At the start of every lesson he would simply dish out a load of pictures and tell us to quietly study them while he buried himself in his latest car magazine. There was talk that he actually had a girlie mag hidden inside the latest "What Car".

Mr Addis, the science teacher, was quite simply bonkers and I'm sure his lifelong ambition was to blow up the classroom. He always seemed to be battling with the fire extinguisher.

Then there was the headmaster, Mr Davis, who you only ever really saw first thing in the morning at assembly or if you were sent for the dreaded "six of the best". Mr Davis had a collection of assorted plimsolls that he would flex in front of you before deciding which one to use. His idea of a laugh was to warn you: "This is going to hurt you more than it will me - now hold out your hand." Any attempt to pull your hand away at the last minute just prolonged the agony.

Incidentally, the one interesting thing about the school morning assembly was waiting for the thud. At least three mornings a week, the whole school would be halfway through "We plough the fields and scatter" when you would hear the thud. You would look round and some poor wretch was spark out on the floor. It was normally the same two or three lads who you could rely on to keel over after running to school on an empty stomach. By the way, it was genuinely years before I twigged that "We plough the fields and scatter" didn't mean "We plough the fields and leg it!"

At one end of the school, hidden behind a wall, was what looked like a big old house where Dickens' Miss Haversham might have once lived. Overgrown with weeds and other garden type stuff that I'm not familiar with, it genuinely looked like a haunted house. This building was, in fact, a school that supplied education for kids with special needs. In those unenlightened times, on a good day we called the kids backward, but they were usually referred to as 'the nutters behind the wall'. It was certainly a no-go area, so if the football went over the wall, it stayed there.

Every few months, one or two of the more unsavoury pupils, if that's not too strong a word, would attempt to set fire to the school with varying degrees of success. It's fair to say that nobody managed to burn the school down, but it certainly didn't stop them trying.

One time the school decided to hold a boxing competition and Anthony Healey, thick as he was, immediately saw the chance to once again turn the screw. Now, my dad was mad on boxing, it was his favourite sport. He told lots of stories about representing the army during the War and a tiny cup sitting proudly on top of the telly bore witness to the fact that he had enjoyed some success. Every other weekend after the pub had closed, he would regale me and my mum with the legendary story of his father, Arthur "Boy" Owen. According to the old man Boy Owen was the greatest and most famous boxer ever to come out of Bradford, Manchester. He was said to be the youngest man ever to top the bill at the well-known Belle Vue boxing venue. The story, told proudly by my dad, was that Boy Owen was due to fight his main featherweight rival for the right to take on the British Champion. Apparently, my paternal grandad, who died before I was born, had been working down Bradford Pit all day, which was hardly ideal preparation for the biggest fight of his life.

The fight, according to dad was a sell-out, no holds barred, no quarter asked or given, a punch-for-punch affair. After 15 gruelling rounds, the referee could not decide on a winner so he made the two shattered gladiators fight one more deciding round. He then awarded victory to the other bloke and, according to my dad, the crowd went mad, fights broke out and chairs were thrown into the ring. Boy Owen was carried out of the arena on the shoulders of adoring fans and was a hero. People talked of nothing else for months. That is how my dad told it, word for word, he never, ever deviated. I made the mistake of sharing this story with the rest of the class - including Anthony Healey.

Many years later, thanks to the internet, I was able to learn the truth about Arthur "Boy" Owen. He was indeed a boxer, but, as far as I could gather, he only ever had one fight and was knocked out in the first round. I cling to the notion that perhaps the man mentioned on the internet was a different Boy Owen and my dad was telling the truth all along. Well, you never know.

Anyway, back to the Grange Street boxing competition. At school, the kids would regularly poke fun at my dad because he was so small and I would always remind them that he was a champion boxer in the army. This was all the ammo that Healey needed, taunting me that, because I came from such a great boxing family, I would have to be a yellow belly if I didn't enter the competition. What I should have said to Healey was "If you do it, so will I". Knowing that he only picked on kids half his size, that would have been the end of it, but sadly, I didn't think of that particular reply until about ten years later.

Come the day of the big boxing gala, I was in a similar situation to that of Boy Owen - he had spent the day working down the pit whilst I hadn't slept for a week worrying about getting my block knocked off.

To decide who should fight who, all the kids were lined up side by side and it was all worked out by height. I was just about the smallest, so obviously I should fight the second smallest. Now, all the other short arses had wisely decided to give this competition a wide berth, so I found myself lined up to fight a boy who was quite a bit taller than me, and, very much like the real Boy Owen story, my first and only attempt at proper boxing ended in first-round humiliation. But at least it kept Anthony Healey off my back for a week or so. I never told my dad about the boxing competition because he would have insisted on putting me through my paces and he would have been bitterly disappointed when I told him I'd been clobbered in the first round.

Ironically, I did get quite interested in boxing around this time, or rather, I became fascinated by the great Cassius Clay, floating like a butterfly and stinging like a bee, so my dad took me to the local boys' club with the idea that I could take up boxing. Bearing in mind the run-ins I'd had with Healey, this might have been a good idea, but apparently I was too young for the boxing. However, I was told I was welcome to join anyway and take part in five-a-side football and table tennis. That was fine by me.

One time, during the run-up to the general election, the school decided to have its own election, but this was only for 4th formers. Me and Tex Hall were still in the 3rd form, so we moaned, complained and played holy hell until we were reluctantly allowed to join in. So, added to the Labour Party, the Tories and the Liberals was the Young People's Party - basically Johnny Owen and Tex Hall. Our manifesto consisted of nine-week summer holidays instead of six and free frozen jubblies every day. On polling day, Tex delivered a rousing speech that, as I remember, got the standing ovation it deserved and the Young People's Party ended up coming a close second to Labour. We also campaigned successfully for a school radio station, which broadcast every Monday for half an hour. I would host the show and Tex and one or two other boys would report on the stories of the week. Not for one moment did I realise that this half hour once a week would end up shaping my adult life. The pop-up radio station actually got a mention on the local Granada news programme "People and Places", and I was invited to appear on the programme and give my opinion on the proposed Comprehensive School that had been given the go-ahead to be built not far from Grange Street. This was one of the first such schools in Britain and was described as "state of the art". I was asked to compare my dilapidated old school with the posh new one, and I decided to focus on Grange Street's leaky old outside toilets and my quote was: " Our conveniences just aren't convenient." Well, at least it got me on the telly and on the same show that the Beatles had made their TV debut a few weeks earlier.

Talking about the Beatles ...

CHAPTER FIVE: "Do Wah Diddy Diddy" Manfred Mann, 1964 (Number One)

It was 1964 and Britain was leading the way in pop music. Brilliant pop groups dominated the charts: The Beatles, The Stones, The Kinks, The Hollies, Manfred Mann – the list goes on.

I was a big Beatles fan right from the off. Every Saturday night my uncle Jack would come around to our house with his girlfriend and play records on my Dansette record player while my mum and dad went to the pub. I really looked up to Jack, he was my hero. He was a decent footballer who once had a trial for Bolton Wanderers, he played the guitar and he had a good looking mini-skirted girlfriend. I called him uncle because I assumed he was my dad's younger brother, but years later my mum told me that in fact he was my cousin, because even though he'd been brought up as the son of dad's mother and father he was in fact the illegitimate offspring of my dad's sister, Auntie Emily. I never liked Auntie Emily or her toffee-nosed husband and I hated their son Thomas. Tom was the same age as me, but we had nothing in common. The wuss didn't even like football. I remember one year my mum bought him a cowboy outfit for Christmas - the Hat, the Sheriff's badge. two guns with holsters, the lot. I was so jealous, especially when I opened Emily's present - a selection box. I remember the night Jack and his girl came round and told me about his new favourite group. He put the record on the Dansette record player, and it was The Beatles' first single Love Me Do. Mum had bought me the Dansette for my birthday, probably from a local shop called Stewart's, where you could buy just about anything and pay for it on what they used to call the 'never-never'. The man would come round every Friday for the weekly instalment. I remember one Friday afternoon my dad and a few of his mates had knocked off work early, gone down the pub, then back to our house to continue the drinking. They were having a good old singsong when the man from Stewart's knocked on the door. I'm not sure there is anything worse than being stone cold sober in a room full of drunkards and the poor man had his money bag confiscated and was held hostage until he agreed to give a rendition of "I Left My Heart in San Francisco". For weeks afterwards, my dad would hide in the kitchen every Friday when he called. My Dansette record player was my pride and joy. With my birthday money I bought two records: one was 'Telstar' by The Tornados and the other was 'Venus in Blue Jeans' by Mark Winter. I opened the front door, sat on the doorstep and played those two records over and over again, until my dad threatened to throw the record player, the records and me "through the bleedin' window."

The downside of Jack coming round on a Saturday was that I was banished into the kitchen all night while he got down to some serious snogging with his girlie. I used to get a couple of socks, roll them into a ball, stick some Sellotape round them and play football all night, United v Arsenal in the FA Cup Final. I remember one might the socks landed on top of our kitchenette. Again, you need to be of a certain age, but two-tone kitchenettes were all the rage back then. They had a shelf in the middle that opened out, so I climbed on the shelf to retrieve the socks, and the whole thing came crashing down on top of me. Self-raising flour, sugar, Ovaltine, you name it, I was covered in it.

I think I got a bit of a good hiding that night when my parents came home and saw the mess, but to be honest, I was used to it. Dad would regularly give me a clip round the ear and send me to bed on a Saturday for letting the fire go out. I never dobbed our Jack in and never told my mum or dad that I had been locked in the kitchen all night and that was why the fire had gone out. Like I said, Jack was my hero.

Dad tolerated The Beatles but he hated The Stones. "Long-haired layabouts," that kind of thing. One time, because I was annoyed with my dad and despite preferring The Beatles, I joined The Rolling Stones fan club, just to annoy him and, boy, did it work! About this time, I decided to get in on the pop scene and form my own group. My mate Jimmy Dinsdale was invited to join because he had a drum. The fact that it was a Salvation Army big bass drum was not ideal but it was by far the best we could do, to this day I have no idea where he got it from. Alan Davies had an acoustic guitar which sadly he couldn't play, but he could bang on the side of it, so he was in. The third member was chosen because he had an instrument, and he could play it. He was even in a local brass band. I can never remember his name, but he was a dab hand on the cornet, the only problem was, all he could play was 'Onward, Christian Soldiers'. Still, it was a start. Then there was me on lead vocals and maracas. When I say maracas, they were really two Sarsons' vinegar bottles painted black and filled with lentils, but I defy anybody to tell the difference. We practised in our front room, when the adults were out, naturally, and convinced ourselves that we were not half bad. We needed to get out there and show people what we were made of. As Christmas 1964 was fast approaching and the lads club was organising a Christmas Eve disco, I somehow managed to talk the committee into letting us play live. "Just one song, that's all, people will love it, honest," I said. Amazingly, they agreed without too much fuss.

There was a group in the charts at the time called The Mojos who we quite liked, so we decided to call ourselves The Lucky Charms. We were fairly chuffed with that, but my Uncle Jack had other ideas. He came up with the fantastic name "3 Dots and a Dash". Wow! How great is that? With a name like that what could possibly go wrong, we were surely on our way to international stardom?

Come the big night and nerves began to get the better of us, although I was still supremely confident, even though our cornet player was throwing up in the toilets. Eight o' clock on Christmas Eve and time to hit the stage. "Boys and girls," said one of the committee members, "Please welcome, for the first time anywhere in the world, The Lucky Charms!" "Psst," I whispered, "Sorry, but we've changed our name, we're now called 3 Dots and a Dash." "Just get on with it," he said, before jumping off the stage.

Picture the scene, if you will, about seventy totally uninterested half-wits in the audience, and Jimmy Dinsdale counts us in, "2-3-4," and starts banging on his Salvation Army bass drum. Alan Davies tries to catch up by banging on his acoustic guitar which, incidentally, by now had no strings, anyway. The bag of nerves cornet player is offering a faultless version of 'Onward, Christian Soldiers' and I start waving my Sarsons' vinegar bottles about like a man possessed, while shouting: "There she was just a-walking down the street, singing Do Wah Diddy Diddy Dum Diddy Do." There was a noise coming from the floor, but it didn't quite sound like applause. Basically, that was the first and last public appearance by 3 Dots and a Dash, and the end of my fledgling pop music career.

One time, Mr McMullen set the class a challenge. We should write to a famous person, asking a question or some advice, and see what sort of reply we got. Of course, I had to take it a stage further and decided to write to every manager in the first division to ask them about their most embarrassing moment on a football field. Out of the twenty-two managers I wrote to, only two bothered to reply. Jimmy Hill, who was then the high-profile manager of Coventry City, sent a lovely type-written letter about the time he missed an open goal and someone in the crowd shouted, "Hill, you bloody chinless wonder!" This made Jimmy's team mates crack up because, if you remember, Jimmy was virtually all chin. Indeed, Jimmy Hill was just about the only bearded man that my dad could abide. He normally hated all men with beards, but he made an exception because "Jimmy needed it to hide his chin". The second letter arrived a few days later. A sprawling two-page, hand-written note on lined paper from the one and only Matt Busby. It related to some tale about the players lining up before kick-off, but nobody had thought to bring a ball. Now, my poor memory might be playing tricks on me here, but I'm sure the letter was written in red ink. Again, not a great story, but this was a hand-written, personally-addressed letter to me from Matt Busby. By this time, I'd been forced to change the name of Denlaw FC to Bradford Athletic because the Man City fans in the team had been kicking up a fuss. To this day, I wish I'd stuck to my guns. However, the following Sunday I decided to make the United fans in the team sick with jealousy by showing them the letter from Busby. After getting my kit together and just before leaving the house I started to look for the letter, but it had vanished. "Mam," I shouted, "Where's my Matt Busby letter?" Her reply was positively nonchalant. She explained that she assumed I'd finished with it, so she'd thrown it on the fire. My hand-written letter from the greatest manager of all time, up in flames. Cheers, Mam.

The idea of writing to the managers may have persuaded Mr McMullen that I might have been a lad worth taking an interest in. That and the poems and plays and stuff. He had a brother who was quite an influential figure in the Droylsden Little Theatre, a well-respected am-dram organisation with headquarters just a mile or so away from our house. He took me along one evening, introduced me to his brother and left, saying this is something you might enjoy. Thinking about it later, I should and would have enjoyed it if I hadn't been so tongue-tied and nervous. It was one thing showing off in front of my class mates, but these people were almost professionals and they seemed ever so posh. They didn't talk about football or what was on the telly last night, in fact I had no idea what they were going on about, I didn't understand a word of it. One chap even had a cigarette holder, and this was some years before Bet Lynch turned up in Corrie using one. I didn't actually realise it was a cigarette holder at the time, I assumed the bloke had got his cigarette caught in some kind of penny whistle type thing and didn't realise. There was some talk about perhaps including me in that year's production of A Christmas Carol: "Would you like to come along next week and read for the part?" Still no idea what they were talking about, but I just nodded politely. I didn't dare speak in front of all these worthy thespians in case they twigged that I was a complete half-wit who lived in one of the slums down the road. I left the Droylsden Little Theatre that evening with my head spinning and never went back, something else I regret

(Point of Order: can there ever be such a thing as a complete half-wit?)

The Bradford Athletic Football Team, formerly known as Denlaw FC, was by now becoming quite respected in the area. We had acquired, not one, but two managers, Mr Dinsdale, whose son Jimmy (he of the Salvation Army big bass drum) played in goal and Mr Mason, whose son Alan was a midfielder and probably my best mate at the time. I have to say that while Mr Dinsdale was dedicated and committed, if a little ponderous, Mr Mason was the motivator and, as far as I was concerned, just the confidence booster I needed. He was always positive, “Good effort, John” or “Great shot, hard luck,” that kind of thing. Sadly, when it came to his own son, just the opposite was true. “Mason, you’re a disgrace, absolutely useless,” he would scream at the top of his voice. These days, whenever I see that famous old film of Brian Clough barking orders at his Derby County team from the touchline during a training session, I automatically think of Mr Mason and the devastating effect his treatment had on his own son who, in fairness, was one of our better players. One occasion, poor old Alan decided he’d had enough and ran away from home, only to return the following day. It turned out that the poor kid had spent the night on a bench in Piccadilly Gardens.

One Saturday night, we even found ourselves on the front page of the famous old “Football Pink” following a 42-0 win in a cup tie. That particular game was laughable. They kicked off, we took the ball off them, went down the other end and scored. That happened forty-six times in the game, but four of the goals were decreed offside. Their manager had the good grace to say that if it hadn’t been for their goalie, the winning margin would have been considerably higher. Over at Rochdale Football Club, Bob Stokoe had recently taken over as manager, and a few years down the line Bob would famously manage Sunderland as they overcame all the odds to beat the mighty but dirty Leeds United in the FA Cup Final at Wembley Stadium. He had gone on record to say he was keen to sign good young players who had been missed by the big clubs. Well, it seems that somebody from Rochdale Football Club had rung Mr Mason to arrange a game between a Rochdale youth team and Bradford Athletic. The man apparently stressed that this was in no way a trial for any one individual, just a practice match. Nobody on our team viewed it as a practice match, this was one game away from the big time, our golden key to a career as professional footballers: Bring It On!

CHAPTER SIX: "Another Nail in my Heart", Squeeze 1980 (Number 17)

A week or so before the biggest game of my life I started to get a pain in my big toe, like somebody was digging into it with a Stanley knife. Not that I knew what that sensation felt like, but I knew something was far from right. After a quick inspection my mother deemed that I had an in-growing toe nail and needed to make an appointment with the chiropodist. I was relieved to hear this news, a poxy in-growing toe nail, nothing to worry about, surely? Having said that, it was incredibly tender.

So, on the Wednesday before the big game in Rochdale I toddled off with my mum to see the chiropodist, or as I called him, 'the foot doctor bloke'. After much digging and levering and no little blood he wrapped a bandage round my toe and told me to rest up for at least a fortnight and under no circumstances should I put any weight on the foot. "But he's football-mad," said my mum, "He's always kicking a ball about." "Out of the question," said the foot doctor bloke, "Football is off the agenda for the time being." I felt my bottom lip start to quiver, with a few crushing words this total stranger was dead set on ruining my life. What did he know? Anyway, nothing was going to stop me playing in this game.

Mr Dinsdale got the money from somewhere to hire a coach to take players, family, friends and well-wishers the twenty or so miles to Rochdale for this eagerly awaited Saturday morning kick-off. Despite her protestations, my mother agreed to come, as did my dad, surprisingly. Sadly, it was no surprise when on the day of the game dad reckoned that he was in so much pain with his back he could not stand the thought of travelling all the way to Rochdale. He was best off staying in bed and resting. My Auntie Ethel volunteered to take Dad's place on the coach, but Ethel, Mum and me knew the real reason the old man couldn't get out of bed - too many pints of Chester's Mild the night before. The players had a good old sing song on the coach as we made our way through Ashton-under-Lyne via Hyde, Royton, through Oldham and deep into the foothills of the South Pennines, to the home of the industrial revolution, Rochdale.

"We love you, Bradford, we do,
We love you, Bradford, we do,
We love you, Bradford, we do,
Bradford Athletic, we love you."

"We hate Nottingham Forest,
We hate Liverpool, too,

We hate Coventry City,
But, Bradford, we love you."

When the Rochdale team came out of the dressing room, we were surprised at how tall they all were. Surprised, but not daunted, after all, most of the teams we played that season were taller than us and we normally sent them home with their tails between their legs. This lot, however, also looked a good three or four years older than the 14-year-olds we normally played against.

The game kicked off and within 30 seconds I had the ball on the left - completely useless with my left foot, my only option was to cut inside. Without thinking, I hit a speculative shot from just outside the penalty area which sailed beautifully into the top corner of the net: Rochdale 0 Bradford Athletic 1. Had the game really started or was I back home still in bed and dreaming it all? No, it was really happening and I was the man of the moment. A couple of minutes later I felt as if I had accidentally stepped into a bucket of water with my right boot. Squelch, squelch, squelch was all I could hear. I had to ease my football boot off and investigate, only to get the shock of my life. It was like a scene from Emergency Ward Ten, only in technicolour. Blood shot out from my big toe like a fountain. Mr Mason's mate, a lovely old chap called Mr Byrd, offered to drive me, my mum and Ethel to Rochdale Infirmary where I spent the next two hours having the offending toe nail removed. I was later told we had lost the game 4-3 but had been far from humiliated. However, as it turned out, none of us heard a peep from Rochdale Football Club ever again. So there you have it, a glittering football career cut short in it's infancy by an in-growing bloody toe nail - bloody being the operative word.

One bank holiday weekend, a few members of the team had the bright idea of going camping in Blackpool, I think it was Joey Walton who came up with the idea. He knew somebody who would lend us a tent. Alan Mason was game, as was Billy Mellor. I definitely wanted to go, but I would have to tell my parents a little white lie. No, make that a whopping great lie. A lie on a par with anything Pinocchio ever dreamed up. I told Mum and Dad that Alan Mason's parents were going to Blackpool for the weekend and they said I could go with them. We would all be safe and warm in a nice cosy guest house and they would pay. The last bit about them paying was enough to convince my dad, and mum couldn't really come up with an argument against it, so I got the all-clear to go. Mum would, of course, give me some money so that the Masons weren't totally out of pocket. I think Alan told his parents the same story, only substituting his parents for mine.

We got the coach to Blackpool and hit the beach at lunchtime on the

Saturday. We did all the things that let-loose teenagers did in Blackpool back then. Quick game of footie on the beach with a cheap lightweight ball that kept blowing into the sea, wind up the aging deck chair attendant, we had some rock, some candy floss, a bag of chips, a bit more rock, followed by a couple of hours in the Fun House. We spent most of the evening walking up and down the beach until somebody mentioned that the tide was coming in. Suddenly Joey Walton started jumping up and down like a demented frog and began running as if for his life. Joey was a good lad and a very decent footballer but not the sharpest tool in the box. He really thought that the tide coming in meant the water actually came up from underneath the sand. It was decided to go and find a field somewhere and erect this tent. By this time, it was pitch black and we had no idea where we might find a suitable field. Incidentally, none of us had a clue as to how to put up a tent. We did eventually find a bit of grass that we thought might be suitable and we set about the tent, just as it started pissing down. After a good hour wrestling with this borrowed tent and getting absolutely nowhere, Bill mentioned that he thought it was far too small to fit all four of us in. Oops, never thought of that. By this time, we were totally soaked through and decided to give up on the camping idea and try to find somewhere under cover to get our heads down for the night. I have no idea how we came to be huddled together in a bus shelter in a deserted country lane, but it was just about the only option open to us by then. This would be our home for the night. We passed the time chatting and joking, inbetween trying and failing to doze off. We tried to pick our greatest ever footballing XI. To this day, I remember arguing with Bill Mellor, who even now is a devoted Man City season ticket holder who never misses a game, that Besty was on a different planet to Mike Summerbee. Come on, Bill, after all these years, admit it.

As daybreak dawned, we were all feeling a little bit peckish and we needed to find a shop that was open. Realistically, there wouldn't have been much chance of that in the centre of Manchester, a shop open at six o'clock in the morning on a Sunday, and we were in the middle of nowhere. Joey and Alan decided to go one way and me and Bill would go in the opposite direction and we would meet "back here in half an hour". Little did I know that me and Bill would never see that bus shelter again. We walked and walked down this meandering country lane. By now it had stopped raining, the birds were singing, and the sun was trying to come out. Bill said it looked like it was going to be a very nice day. Bill, bless him, had spoken too soon. We came to a small row of large detached houses. No one was stirring, the lights were off, everybody still sensibly tucked up in their beds. Then we noticed two bottles of milk on one of the doorsteps. "Oh, the milkman's been," said Bill. If we helped ourselves to the milk then found a shop selling cornflakes, that was breakfast sorted. We tiptoed down the drive, carefully and as quietly as we could, picked up the milk bottles and tiptoed back up the drive. Suddenly Bill shouted "Run" and started racing off. "What's up with him," I thought, then a police car screeched to a halt and we were dragged by the scruff of our scrawny necks into the back of the car. "Under arrest for stealing two bottles of milk," said the policeman. The very first thing I thought to myself was, "My dad is going to wipe the floor with me."

We spent most of that lovely warm Sunday locked in a police cell just outside Blackpool feeling very sorry for ourselves until finally the door was unlocked and we were told to stand up. Two very stern looking police officers told us to follow them. As we got to the front door of the police station, we saw a patrol car with the engine running and the back doors open. Suddenly police issue overcoats were thrown over our heads and we were dragged to the car. "Jesus," I thought, "They take a dim view of milk thieves round here." By now, I was totally bricking it, this was the kind of thing you see on the news when suspected murderers have been arrested. Maybe the householder was watching the entire milk theft through his window and had a heart attack and died. Now they were trying to pin a murder charge on us. The two policemen must have been chuckling fit to burst as they went through this ridiculous charade. They were actually driving us to the coach park. They had verified that we had given our correct names and addresses, the householder didn't want to press charges, so we were free to go. "We were just teaching you a lesson, lads," smiled one of the coppers. Lesson learnt, officer, now comes the real fly in the ointment: "What the hell is my dad going to say, and, more importantly, do about this shambolic episode?"

I didn't have long to wait. They were both waiting for me when I dragged myself through the door. I explained that I was shattered and just wanted to go to bed. Nice try, but no chance. Putting to one side the lies I had told about Mr and Mrs Mason, "And by the way," said my mum "Alan won't be allowed out for a good while." How could I bring shame on the family by stealing milk from a penniless old-aged pensioner? "What old-aged pensioner?" I asked. "There's a lot of old people live in Blackpool," screamed my dad, "With not a lot of money, and you decide to go stealing their milk!" For a few seconds, I couldn't help looking round at our tiny terraced hovel, a couple of steps up from The Beverly Hillbillies pre-windfall shack, and comparing it to the large detached villa in Blackpool, although I thought it best to keep quiet. Amazingly, my dad didn't lay a hand on me. Maybe he took in the pathetic bleary-eyed state I was in and felt a bit sorry for me. There was a lot of shouting and threatening but I was eventually sent to bed to "Think on". That was fine by me, I could have slept for England.

The tale of the working-class housewife becoming infuriated by her husband staying in the pub rather than coming home for his tea, or dinner, is a bit of an old chestnut. You know the story, she finally runs out of patience and storms round to the pub and plonks the meal on the bar before walking out. Well, my mum did that on more than one occasion. One Saturday in particular, Dad said he was going to put a bet on, then he was nipping for a pint and he'd be back in about an hour. That would have been about mid-day. By seven o'clock there was still no sign of him, and his lamb chops were in danger of turning to charcoal. By eight o'clock she was at the end of her tether, she'd had enough of being taken advantage of by that selfish little so and so. She took the plate out of the oven, wrapped it in a tea towel and marched off down the street towards the Duke of Edinburgh. No sign of dad, although a few of the regulars volunteered to take the food off her hands. No sign in the Grey Mare, either, but yet again plenty of people willing to wolf down the meal on his behalf. Strangely, he hadn't been seen in the Swan with Two Necks all day, but one chap told mum he'd seen him in the Old Vic earlier. She'd walked past the Old Victoria Inn to get to the Grey Mare but hadn't thought to go in. Yet there he was, holding court in the snug. Mum slung down the plate in front of a giggling excuse for a husband and father, whipped off the tea towel and walked out. "That'll teach him," she thought. "Show him who's boss." She should have known better after all these years. By midnight he still hadn't come home. "Bone Idle Piss Pot," she mumbled, as she turned the lights out and went to bed. It was gone half past one when an almighty clatter woke us both up as dad crashed through the door. He was in a terrible state. A bloody nose, blood coming from his mouth, trousers ripped at the knees and his false teeth missing. "What the bloody hell?" said my mother. I can't quite remember in what order dad tried to describe what had happened, but it went something like: "Bleedin' bastard bleeder crept up on me. Just walking home, minding my own business. Bleedin' bastard jumped me, I know who did it, the bleedin' bastard, I know who did it. all right. Just walking home and he jumped me, I'll get our Bill round and some of the lads, he won't know what's hit him, bleedin' bastard."

The next morning Dad, who by now looked like he'd gone ten rounds with Henry Cooper, was still determined to get his brother Bill and "a few of the lads" round to sort out this cowardly assailant when there was a knock at the door. It was a lady from two streets away. She handed a handkerchief to my mum and began telling the story. She had been woken first by the singing in the early hours of the morning. Dad had staggered into the middle of the road singing his head off when he was sent flying by a bloke on either a motor bike or moped. The lady could see his false teeth come hurtling out of his mouth. As dad lay motionless on the ground, the chap on the motor bike or moped checked to see that he wasn't dead, then drove off. Then Dad staggered to his feet and tottered on his way, this time without the singing. The lady had thoughtfully retrieved his dentures and wrapped them in a hankie, which my mum was now holding.

Don't think I'd ever seen the old man looking so sheepish.

The regular slaps and punches off Anthony Healey were now becoming almost a daily occurrence. Virtually every playtime he would push me into the school railings or trip me up and kick me while I was on the ground. One lunchtime, during our regular ad-hoc football matches, Healey made a challenge on another lad, I instinctively shouted "Foul" and I knew immediately it was a big mistake. Healey turned and walked menacingly towards me, his face contorted with anger and hate, his fist clenched. I looked round at Mr Addis who was on playground duty, hoping he would intervene, but before I knew it Healey was standing over me and punched me full in the face with all his might. I hit the ground and the back of my head split open. I started sobbing, not so much out of pain, more out of shock. I looked at Mr Addis, the science teacher who saw it all happen, but he was doing nothing. I thought he would at least drag Healey to the headmaster's office, but no, he never said a word. Maybe because Mr Addis was only a slightly built man, he himself was wary of Healey, or whether he thought I deserved it, I'll never know, but these days somebody would have recorded it on a mobile phone, put it on YouTube, and it would have gone viral, the media would have been outraged, an organisation would be set up to send me abroad to recover and a "Justice for Johnny" charity would be set up to "put an end to bullying once and for all". But back then, nothing. Even the teachers couldn't be arsed.

But Healey's comeuppance was heading his way.

CHAPTER SEVEN: **"Eleanor Rigg(by)", The Beatles 1966 (Number One)**

A new girl round our way was causing quite a stir for a number of reasons. First of all, she was very good-looking, and she knew it. Also, she had a cleavage! Don't think any of the other girls in our immediate circle had one between them. She wore miniskirts and white knee length socks. All the lads called them "virgin socks", no idea why. I'm pretty sure that all the 14-year-old girls in Bradford were virgins at the time, as indeed were the lads, so I'm not sure their choice of hosiery made any difference. But most of all, it was her name that was causing a commotion. Almost identical to a Beatles number one hit of the day.

"Eleanor Rigby picks up the rice off the floor where the wedding has been,
Lives in a Dream.
Waits at the window,
Wearing a face that she keeps in a jar by the door,
Who is it for?"

One of Macca's finest.

Eleanor Rigg had virtually appeared out of nowhere. She didn't seem to have a mother or father but instead lived with her gran in Score Street just round the corner.

She was certainly a hit with all the lads. Think of Sid James' daughter in "Bless This House" but give her a young Elsie Tanner's voice and you're getting there. One Saturday evening, I had just tucked into my tea when there was a knock at the door. It was a girl about my age. "My mate fancies you," she said, pointing to the gorgeous mini-skirted Miss Rigg, who was peeping round the corner. "She'll meet you in the park tomorrow at two o'clock near the café." So that was it, I had a date, with a girl, and a very good-looking girl at that. I wolfed my tea down, ran out and called for my mate Alan Mason, he would be the first to hear the news. He would be so jealous because he really fancied her as well.

So, there I was in Philips Park on a hot summer's Sunday afternoon making awkward small talk with this fascinating creature. I didn't ask about her exotic Beatle-style name or where she had come from or about her mum and dad. I asked her if she'd seen Batman on the telly the night before. She hadn't. I asked her if she liked football. She didn't. I asked her if she fancied going on the boating lake. She couldn't be bothered. Suddenly she said: "Are you going to kiss me or what?" Now, I'm not going to pretend the thought had never crossed my mind, indeed it's all

I'd thought about since waking up that morning, but if you put aside the Marilyn Pilot fiasco some years earlier, I had never kissed a girl before, I don't think I had even held hands with one, so this was a big step. It needed a coat of thinking about. "Let's have a walk round first," I suggested, playing for time. "Well, if you can't be bothered, I'm going home." Can't be bothered? If she only knew how much I wanted to acquaint myself with those ruby red lips. I don't know what provoked her to say what she said next, maybe it was the desperate look on my face or maybe she had read exactly what was on my mind. "Is it because I'm taller than you?" In truth, Eleanor Rigg was a fair bit taller than me and, yes, the idea of stretching to make contact was more than a little off-putting. After all these years, I'm not sure what happened next ever really happened, but bizarre as it sounds, I do have a memory of wandering off in search of a couple of bricks to stand on. Whatever the circumstances, I did end up giving her a kiss, and a long, lingering kiss at that. Half way through I did briefly open my eyes to gauge if she was in the same blissful state as I was. Disappointingly, her eyes were wide open staring back at me. Putting that to one side, I was delighted with my afternoon's work and from then on there was no stopping me, I was an absolute kissing machine.

For the next few weeks, playing football suddenly held no real interest for me, my mates were largely ignored and all I cared about was getting to grips with my stunning new girlie. We were allowed to be alone in her gran's parlour every night until I was chucked out at nine o'clock. The first time I entered the house, I was shocked. It was like going back in time. All the furniture was at least 50 years old and covered in dust, there was no electricity in the house, gas mantles only. So that's why she hadn't watched Batman! The word 'eerie' doesn't really cover it. But there was a bigger shock to come. One night when we were in our usual deep erotic clinch, I heard a strange noise, which I assumed was a leaky gas mantle. "A gas leak," I shouted. "We'd better get out of here." Eleanor laughed, "It's not a gas leak," she said. "The snake must have come downstairs." Snake? First I'd heard of a snake. She went to the bottom of the stairs and scooped up the hideous-looking reptile. "Say hello to Goldie," she smiled. Amazingly, even that didn't put me off, the kissing and cuddling continued unabated – until...

One evening, I knocked on as usual and her gran told me she had gone back to live with her parents - in Carlisle. "Fancy not saying goodbye," was my first thought. I never saw or heard from Eleanor Rigg ever again, so it was back to my mates and football every night. The kissing had to stop sometime, I suppose, but while it lasted, it was certainly an eye-opener, no pun intended.

One Friday afternoon, I was being chased through the streets by Anthony Healey. Nothing unusual about that, it was a fairly regular occurrence. I can't for the life of me recall what was bugging the great big lump of uselessness on this occasion, but he certainly seemed more crazed than ever. Now, I have never been a fighter, but I could run and I made it through the front door of our house just before he attempted to kick it in. Little did either of us know it at the time, but that particular Friday afternoon was the beginning of the end of my problems with Healey. I think when he tried to kick the door down he assumed that my parents were at work, but sadly for him my mum was home. She opened the door and a snarling Healey screamed, "I'll fuckin' kill him next time I see him." Mum gave as good, if not far better, than she got and Healey skulked off like the miserable worm he was. "Mum, you're making it worse for me," was my initial reaction, but she sat me down and wanted to know what had been going on. Normally, I would have just brushed it off as a playground tiff but by now I was at my wit's end and just wanted it stopped. I told her everything, the time I came home with a black eye and said I'd been hit with a cricket ball, the times I came home with my nose bleeding - they weren't just unexplained nosebleeds. When I came home in tears, I hadn't fallen over. Everything was down to being constantly picked on by Healey. My dad had his usual idea of going round the pubs looking for Healey's father, because a few words over a couple of pints might solve the problem. But my mum was determined to take control. She was taking the day off work on Monday, coming with me to school and sorting this out once and for all.

On the Monday morning we were standing outside the classroom when Healey, not a care in the world, came sauntering up the corridor. I can still clearly see him now briefly stopping in his tracks, taking a deep breath and walking past us, my mum's eyes burning deep into his thick skull. She asked Mr McMullen for permission to speak to the headmaster. Mr Davis listened carefully and was clearly shaken. Now, I don't think for a minute that it was just the bullying, but Healey had form, petty theft, threatening behaviour, vandalism and now he was being unmasked as a serial bully. It was the final straw, he was out: expelled! He was to go on the Friday and the shameless, spineless good-for-nothing arsehole spent the next few days trying to suck up to me in order to somehow save his bacon. No chance, mate. Just get the hell away from me.

During the following Healey-free week, one of his cronies, a lad called Austin, casually asked me if I was glad that Healey had been expelled. I may have replied with something like, "Is the Pope a Catholic?" Of course, Healey had put him up to asking the question and what I didn't realise was that Healey's bad reputation meant that no school in the area would entertain the idea of taking him, so he was free to wander the streets all day thinking of ways to do me harm. One day, I spotted the slimy git hanging around outside the school gates obviously waiting for four o'clock and the chance to do me a bit more damage. As there was only one way in and one way out of the school, I was in a bit of a pickle, so I went to see the headmaster who amazingly organised police protection for me. A bobby on a bicycle (ask your grandad, kids) walked me home every afternoon for three days, before they either got fed up or decided I was in no real danger.

One day I wandered out of school and was making my way home when I sensed that somebody was running after me. I looked round and it was him, Anthony Healey. He just wouldn't let it go. My first instinct was to run for my life, but after a few yards I thought "Do you know, I have really had enough of this," and I turned round to face him. Before I knew it, I was actually grappling in the street with my worst nightmare and briefly, very briefly, getting the better of him. I had him in a headlock, and he was struggling to free himself. I looked at his head, it was at my mercy, and I looked at the nearby wall. I could ram his head as hard as I could against the wall and that might slow him down. But what if it didn't? What if it just made him madder? While I was contemplating all this, he grabbed my hair, pulled me down to my knees and kicked me full in the face. Just then, an old chap came rushing over to admonish Healey and he walked away. And guess what? I never saw him again. By fighting back I think he realised that it wasn't fun anymore. Over the years, I instilled in my son Marc that if he was ever being bullied, just stand up and fight back. I wish I had done that an awful lot sooner, it would have saved me many a sleepless night.

Eleanor Rigg aside, I was never much cop with the girls. Most of my knowledge regarding the female anatomy was gleaned from my mum's Kay's catalogue, pages 201-237, the ladies' undergarments section. "Can I borrow your catalogue, Mam?" I would say, "I want to look at the toys 'n' stuff." Like hell I did. The bra and knickers collection was where it was at. "Nurse, the screens." I do remember mum and Auntie Angie coming back to our house unexpectedly one afternoon to find me in my bedroom canoodling Josie Rowe. Mum went completely spare, threatening to tell my dad and calling me a "dirty little so-and-so", while Angie just giggled on the settee. I was 15 at the time and it was only a bit of kissing and clueless fondling. Then there was Sharon Parker, a lovely-looking girl that I "pinched" off Alan Mason. Sadly we had a big row one day about who was the best, the Beatles or the Monkees. I mean, come on, the Monkees were OK but I just couldn't go out with a girl who thought they were better than The Fab Four. Susan Mercer was another girl I quite liked. We were very close for a while, so close that I spent almost the entire six-week summer holiday trying to undo her bra. I gave up in the end and bought a football. Another girl called Lynn Powell who lived round the corner seemed to have "gone out" with most of my mates and she had a bit of a reputation, but she had no interest in me. I used to think, "She was kissing Jimmy Dinsdale last night and I'm better looking than him!" One day I lay on the ground next to her house and pulled my bike on top of me to make it look like I'd fallen off and hurt myself. Then I waited for her to come home and feel sorry for me. I waited and waited. When she eventually did show up, she nonchalantly stepped over me and the bike, walked into her house and slammed the door without a second glance. I genuinely think that if I hadn't stumbled into dee-jaying, I would probably still be a virgin. When you were the dee-jay the girls usually made the first move, even if it was just to ask for a record. Making the first move was always impossible for me.

When the letter from the council dropped through the door to say that our house and the rest of the houses in Moody Street were to finally be demolished, I was over the moon. I was embarrassed by the area and the house itself. Mum had done her very best over the years to keep it clean and tidy, but the truth is, like every other house in the area, it was an outdated slum, over-run by cockroaches. If you got up in the night, went down stairs and turned the light on the little (or not so little) bastards scattered to all four corners. Going to the toilet was also deeply humiliating, out in the back yard, no light and just a few torn up pieces of the Manchester Evening News on a piece of string behind the door posing as toilet paper. I remember when I was about ten years old going to see the film Pollyanna starring Hayley Mills. Not my kind of film at all, but I sat through it twice because of her house. I never in my wildest dreams imagined that anybody could live in a beautiful house like that. Leaving the cinema and having to go back home was severely depressing. I suspect my mum felt the same, but my dad was reluctant to leave. After all, his favourite pubs were all within walking distance as was Eva Brothers Limited. He could stagger out of bed at ten to eight in the morning and be there in ten minutes. A couple of years ago I joined a Facebook site for people who were born and bred in Bradford, Manchester and virtually all the members feel proud and grateful to have grown up in those grotty two-up and two-down slums. Much as I enjoy reliving the memories, I can't share their nostalgia for the houses or the area.

Before moving house, it was time to think about getting a job. I was 15 years old and there was never a discussion about staying on for another year or going to college, I was expected to start bringing a wage into the house. My mum took me to Burton's the Tailor on Piccadilly to be measured up for a navy-blue pinstriped suit, very smart, and something I would need for any interviews. Once again, Mr McMullen tried his best to help, he thought I had the makings of a decent journalist so arranged for me to be interviewed at the Daily Express. Why nobody thought that it might be a good idea to start off at a small provisional newspaper I will never know, but here I was donning my new suit and preparing to go to the prestigious offices of the Daily Express. I can't remember too much about the interview apart from being told that my first months would be spent making the tea and sweeping the floor. Well, that was no good to me, if I was to be a journalist, I wanted to get on with it. I quite fancied being sent to watch a United game or at the very least Oldham Athletic. Making the tea and sweeping the floor was a total waste of my talents. I went home and told my mum that I had no intention of being a tea boy or a sweeper-upper. A few days later my mum noticed an advert in the Evening News for a junior sales assistant at Burton's on Piccadilly, the very same place I'd been measured for my suit just a few weeks earlier. I remember being very impressed with Burton's, all the staff were very smart and incredibly civilised. No heavy lifting involved and, unlike my dad, I wouldn't be coming home every night looking dirty and filthy and needing a good scrubbing. When I told Mr McMullen that I had got a job as a shop assistant the look of disappointment on his face was all too clear.

CHAPTER EIGHT: "Dedicated Follower of Fashion", The Kinks 1966 (Number 4)

My mum had taken the morning off work to make doubly sure I was presentable, washed behind the ears, with no sign of a tide mark. In my eyes, I was dressed to kill in my brand-new made-to-measure pin-striped suit, purchased for me on the never-never from the very same store where, very soon, I would be starting my working life. I joined the queue for the 216 bus to Piccadilly, and what a queue it was. Three buses came and went, full to bursting, and I was still nowhere near getting on. The concept of a rush hour was a new one on me and I'd failed to take it into account.

Mum had warned me about being polite, and not speaking until I was spoken to. "Yes, sir, no, sir, three bags full, sir," but she never mentioned the rush hour. Perhaps because her and my dad both worked a five-minute walk from our house, it probably never occurred to her, either. Thinking about it, most people worked just a few minutes away from where they lived. I reckon I might have been the first person in our family to get the bus to work. The thought of being late on my first day was now bringing me out in a sweat, the sort of musty, salty sweat that only teenagers seem to get and the sort of sweat that left a grubby line round your crisp white shirt collar. "Oh my God," I thought, "If I ever get there, I'll be sent straight back home for being a scruffy little sod."

Eventually I was able to scramble onto a packed 216 double decker and we slowly, but surely, headed towards Manchester city centre - standing room only, but who cares? Half a mile down the road, the bus suddenly died. I knew immediately what had happened. The 216 was an electric bus that travelled on tram lines, the last of its kind in the North West, and the wire thing that ran from the bus to the tram lines had dropped off. I knew from experience that it happened all the time, but why did it have to happen now?

The bus conductor wearily got his big stick out and reconnected the bus to the lines and off we went. When the bus eventually reached the bus station opposite Piccadilly Gardens, I jumped off and ran for my life the 200 or so yards to Burton's the Tailors. I was met by the manager, a short tubby man with a tape measure around his neck and a biro behind his ear. He tapped his watch, twice to emphasise his point. "It's ten past nine, young man," he said. "You are meant to start at quarter to." In between my gasps for breath, I tried to explain to him that the bus had broken down, but I could tell he didn't believe a word I was saying, and he warned me that it must never happen again before shouting over to another young lad, who had been ear wigging nearby. "Mr Hall," he said, beckoning the lad over. "This is young Mr Owen, he has eventually joined us today, so show him the ropes for the next couple of days."

Back in the late Sixties, Burton's the Tailors was very much like the TV show "Are you Being Served". You had to call your colleagues 'Mister' when you were on the shop floor, whether you were addressing the manager, the assistant manager, the senior sales assistants or a sweaty little nobody like me, and the question, "Are you free?" was genuinely often heard.

I was incredibly impressed with Mr Hall, or Keith as I was allowed to privately call him. He was wearing an ice blue mohair suit with a five-button cuff and a 17" centre vent in his jacket, shiny black brogues and he had a skinhead haircut with a razor parting. In short, he looked and sounded like the trendy soul boy that I would soon aspire to be.

Having just about got my bearings, I was sent on the breakfast run to the local Greek greasy spoon cafe round the corner for toasted tea cakes and bacon sarnies. Over breakfast, although I was too nervous to eat, I discovered that Keith, like me, was mad about football and thankfully a United fan. He was even more enthusiastic about his music. He was really into Motown and Stax records and told me he went to somewhere called the Twisted Wheel on a regular basis. I had no idea what he was talking about, what in God's name was a twisted wheel? For my part, I just smiled, nodded, and tried to give the impression that I was fully up to speed.

Back on the shop floor Keith handed me this contraption and told me to clean the individual compartments that held all the suit trousers and raincoats. I got stuck into this with great gusto, sweeping this new-fangled contraption back and forth until my arm felt like it was about to drop off. My new best mate and a couple of the more senior assistants had been watching me for over half an hour when Keith walked over and said, "You're doing a very decent job there mate, but I think it might be better if you plugged it in." I really just wanted the floor to open up and swallow me whole. I was so embarrassed, my new hero must think I'm a right dimwit. I spluttered that I wasn't really thick, honest, I was just too nervous to think straight. At lunchtime, I was going from the stock room to the kitchen to have the ham butties my mum had prepared for me, when I noticed two women beckoning me from the front door, but I thought I might get another telling off from the manager so I blanked them. I later found out that it was my mum's two sisters, Auntie Ethel and Auntie Angie, who had bought me some fish and chips.

In the afternoon, one of the senior assistants told me to go to the other branch which was on Deansgate for "a Long Stand" so I stood there patiently for over two hours before another bloke in a pin-striped suit with a tape measure round his neck told me they didn't have any Long Stands. I didn't twig until about three months later.

Saturdays at Burton's was bedlam. It was as if every man in Manchester had woken up that morning desperate for a new made-to-measure suit and it must be purchased from Montague Burton's on Piccadilly. These days you just don't hear of men having their suits made to measure but back then it was pretty much the norm. From the moment we opened the doors at nine in the morning until we closed them at six in the evening, the place was jam-packed. A crocodile of men, queuing patiently to be measured for their new whistle and flute, was never ending. There was only one man doing the measuring, old Mr. Hallam, a grumpy, bad-tempered old chap, who seemed to me to be about 125 years old. He was deemed to be too hostile to deal with the public and so was always put on measuring duty, because by the time the punters got to him they had chosen their cloth, chosen their style and paid their deposit, so Mr Hallam did not have to talk to them. He had massive hands on the end of elastic arms, a bit like Inspector Gadget years later. If he thought you were being a bit cheeky, his arm would shoot out and he could give you a stinging clip round the ear from across the room.

I was being paid a measly five pounds seventeen shillings and sixpence for a five-day week - that's just over £5.50 in today's money. It was traditional back in the day to hand over half your first week's wages to your mother, and my mum suggested that I should hand the other half to my Nan because of "everything she had done for me", so for the first week I worked for absolutely nothing. To be honest, my mum had a point and I didn't really mind. You could also earn commission in a couple of ways, one was by selling a suit that somebody had previously had made-to-measure but, for one reason or another, they had failed to collect. The other was what they called 'a double sale', which involved selling somebody a suit, either made-to-measure or readymade, and then selling them what, in those days, was called a car coat, but was basically an overcoat. Either of these methods would earn you 50p commission. I had been watching the other sales assistants going through the double sale procedure all week. The idea was that you sold the suit and then you went and got a car coat in their size and told the customer that this was a new item in stock and would they please try it on and give their opinion. Once they were wearing the coat, you would take them to a mirror and say something like "actually, that really suits sir". More often than not, it didn't result in a sale, but it seemed to me that every single customer was happy to go through the motions.

My first ever customer came half way through the morning, a man, together with his wife and their teenage daughter had wandered in looking for a readymade suit. Amazingly, I made a sale and it was pretty straight forward. In those days everybody paid cash and in future months that would lead to a very nice little earner for me, but for now, as I made my way to the cashier's booth, I was just happy to have got my name on the score sheet, as it were. As I was waiting for the cashier to process the sale, Mr Riley, the manager, sidled over and whispered, "Don't forget the double sale." So I took a deep breath, pulled a car coat from the rack and did the spiel: "This is a new line we've just got in, we would like to know what our customers think of it, would you mind trying it on, please?" I held the coat out, but the bloke grabbed it, threw it back on the desk, and said: "Don't be cheeky, lad." Well, my bottom lip started quivering, my eyes started watering and the teenage daughter started stifling a giggle. His sympathetic wife tried to comfort me by rubbing my arm, but I brushed her away like a temperamental five-year-old. If I was to succeed in the cut throat world of retail I would certainly have to toughen up.

In the ensuing weeks, I became a bit of a disciple of the stylish Mr Hall, taking in everything he told me about his beloved soul music. Up until now, I was really into the Beatles and the Hollies and the Kinks of this world, but I suddenly found myself searching out the latest releases from the likes of the Temptations, Smokey Robinson and the Miracles, and Sam and Dave. My Dad, of course, got the hump: "Where are you getting all this darkie stuff from, bleedin' rubbish." My dad wasn't prejudiced – he hated everybody. His intolerance stretched from black people, "apart from the great Nat King Cole" to Jewish people, "apart from the great Al Jolson", but he especially despised Mike and Bernie Winters, and all men with beards, although he made an exception with Jimmy Hill "because of his chin". Whenever the hapless Mike and Bernie came on the telly, me and Mum would look at each other and prepare ourselves for the tirade of abuse that my dad would let rip: "Who's keeping these two pillocks in work?" he would shout, not waiting for an answer. "I wouldn't pay 'em in washers."

Apart from his love of soul music and football, Keith was also a keen cricketer, and one evening after work I went to see him play. I don't remember much about the game, but when Keith came to get dressed afterwards somebody had stolen his suit. He had been wearing a made-to-measure eye-catching lime-green mohair suit, which sounds horrendous, but at the time! Well, at the time, I suppose it *was* horrendous but certainly eye-catching. Keith was apoplectic, for one thing he would have still been paying for it on the weekly.

About a week later we were standing at the doorway of Burton's, no doubt clocking the girls, when two young lads walked past, and I recognised one of them immediately: it was Manchester United footballer Brian

Kidd, who had recently achieved legendary status by scoring a goal in the European Cup Final on his 19th birthday. I had no idea who the other lad was, but he was wearing an eye-catching lime green suit! "That's my suit!" spluttered Keith. Brian Kidd and the suspect started running away as Keith gave chase and he beckoned me to "come on". We chased them all round Piccadilly until we eventually lost them. Sometime later, I was watching a game at Old Trafford when I saw Brian Kidd knock the infamous Southampton and former Everton hard man Jimmy Gabriel spark out. As Gabriel lay on the soaking wet Old Trafford turf, seeing nothing but stars, I couldn't help but be relieved that we never caught up with them on that afternoon on Piccadilly.

Before too long, I was dressing much like my new hero. Made to measure mohair suits with a five-button cuff and a 14-inch vent in the jacket. I seemed to be ordering a new suit every month and I developed a strategy that I was convinced had my mum completely fooled. I would take my new suit home and tell my mum that a customer had ordered it but not turned up to claim it. "Can I have it, Mam, please, it fits like a glove?" Years later she told me that she had seen through my ploy from virtually day one, but she went along with it because it made her happy to see me so smart, bless her!

Then one day it happened, Keith Hall casually mentioned that he was going to the Twisted Wheel that night and did I want to come. "Did I want to go to the Twisted Wheel?" I could not have been more excited if he'd asked me to join him on a trip to the moon or play for United. At last, I was going to see for myself just what went on in this legendary Shangri La.

The queue to get in seemed to go on forever, this place must be amazing, why else would all these trendy young men and women about town be so desperate to get in? I really didn't know what to expect, but when I eventually made it inside, I really had to work hard to disguise my disappointment. The Twisted Wheel was clammy, damp and a little bit scary. Well, it was scary to me anyway. Prior to this, my idea of a music venue was the local youth club on a Tuesday night, which was run by a couple of do-gooders doing their bit for the under-privileged community. This was basically a church or school hall, I really can't remember which, with a record player in the corner and half a dozen records to choose from.

I think I'd expected a lot more from the Twisted Wheel or "The Wheel" as all the punters called it - no whistles, no bells, no glamorous dolly birds on unicycles - the place was past its sell-by date, to say the least. But the music was fantastic. This would have been just before the Northern Soul explosion, so the music was Otis Redding, Joe Tex, the Temptations. The first record I ever danced to, or rather attempted to dance to, in the

Wheel was Show Me by Joe Tex, but try as I might to dance like all the other incredibly cool dudes, I couldn't help but notice that I was being stared at - and not in a good way. I may have looked the part in my mohair suit and polo shirt, but I would need to sharpen up on the dance floor. Maybe trying to get to grips with a Joe Tex number was a step too far. Little did I know that many years later the story of Joe being the only pop star to die by being eaten by a bear would become something of a staple of my radio show.

Then came the day I was no longer the Burton's dogsbody, a new rookie would assume that dubious mantle. Enter young Gordon Brownsword, an unkempt gormless-looking 15-year-old, a million miles from the man of the world that I had become. It was now my turn to send young Gordon to the Deansgate branch for a Long Stand, and he had to do the run to the greasy spoon cafe in all weathers for the toasted tea cakes. It was common practice that when a customer called to collect his made-to-measure suit, you would rip the labels off the jacket and trousers. In truth you were supposed to carefully cut the tag with scissors, but nobody ever did. One day I was dealing with such a customer and as I ripped the label off the trousers, I also ripped off the back pocket leaving a great big hole. In panic I looked at the customer, but he was busy browsing the shirts and hadn't noticed. I saw young Mr Brownsword on the shop floor, so I pressed the label against the offending hole and said: "Mr Brownsword, would you mind taking over, it's my break time." With that, I disappeared into the kitchen and left Gordon to face the consequences. In fairness, young Mr Brownsword had been a bit of a walking disaster ever since he started, and the manager decided that this was the last straw. I was genuinely sorry to see him go, mainly because, for the time being at least, I was back on the breakfast run.

When I describe myself as a 'man of the world', I may be stretching a point. One day, I noticed that Keith Hall had started wearing cuff links so I promised myself that next Friday, pay day, I would take myself off to Debenhams for a tiny bottle of Brut aftershave and a pair of cuff links.

I couldn't get my head around the price of cuff links. I mean, I wanted to be in with the in-crowd, but there was a limit. I was obviously getting too big for my brogues, who did I think I was, Charles Clore? Then I noticed some cuff links I could afford, not exactly stylish, and why were there three of them, and why was one so much smaller than the other two? When I got back to Burton's and proudly showed them off to the assistant manager, Mr Howard, I discovered why they were so cheap, why there were three of them and why they were different sizes - they weren't cuff links at all, they were collar studs (ask your grandad, kids). As Mr Howard gleefully shared the joke round the shop, I could have happily curled up and died. Man of the World? Not quite.

Skyscrapers were going up just a few miles away, to house the people whose slums had been demolished, but my mum was adamant that she would not live in a "flat in the sky" and she turned down all offers to do so. Eventually, we settled on a nice little house in the cosmopolitan area of Withington to the south of the city. At last, a home to be proud of, with front and rear gardens, a bathroom and a separate indoor toilet. Yes, an indoor toilet, blessed be the Lord! No central heating, but one mustn't be greedy. Dad was sceptical because it was miles away from his work, two fairly long bus journeys, in fact, and it was miles away from his favourite pubs, but mum was determined to have her own way on this one, and we were definitely moving in to Number 60, Dennison Avenue, Withington. That's right, an avenue - with trees - it was great to smell the grass as opposed to the Tripe Works. As we settled in to our new home, Dad's drinking became worse. He would finish work then go straight into the pub until getting on for ten o'clock at night. On leaving the boozer, no doubt he would have been all 'hail-fellow-well-met', the life and soul of the party, more than happy to get the round in: "A genuine good bloke, that Johnny Owen." Two buses later and by the time he eventually got home, he would be in a filthy mood and all too ready to take it out on Mum, both verbally and physically. One such night, he was especially raging, shouting at Mum, calling her all the names under the sun. Why? No idea. I, as usual, sat on the settee pretending to watch the telly, until he started slapping her across the face. I'd seen it all before, years of it, but tonight I suddenly snapped. I jumped up, pushed him against the wall, grabbed him by the lapels, called him a few names. It was the first and last time I ever swore in front of my parents, but I told him to get to bed and called him pathetic. I fully expected him to turn his anger on me and was ready for the onslaught, but instead he genuinely looked frightened - of me - he tried to laugh it off, but I wasn't fooled. My father, who all his married life had been too fond of hitting out at his wife, was a coward. I genuinely would have thought more of him if he had punched me in the face, but instead he skulked off to bed, and things between us would never be the same again.

Back at Burton's, I had really become a Keith Hall disciple, If he ordered a new made-to-measure mohair suit, then I had to have one, too. Against my mum's specific orders, I went to the same barber as Keith to have a crop haircut with a razor parting. There was only one hairdresser to go to for this particular style, Jack in Shudehill, close to the Jewish quarter of Manchester. Jack was always busy and there would always be a queue of teenage lads eager to have most of their hair cut off. Jack was still cutting hair in the same salon in the Nineties. By this time, Jack himself was almost 90 years old and nearly blind. By then, the poor bloke was getting so many complaints from irate customers that the council tried to have him closed down, but Jack refused to budge, so a compromise was agreed. Jack allowed the council to place a notice in the shop window to the effect that "the owner of this establishment has been certified as legally blind - enter at your own risk".

When my mum first saw my new trendy haircut, she let out a horrified "Yelp" and declared that I looked like I'd just come out of borstal. Looking back, she was probably spot on, but at the time, well, if Keith Hall thought it looked great, so did I.

I decided I needed a Crombie overcoat to complete the look, but as all the Crombies in stock were far too big for little old me, and as I was working for Burton's the Tailor, I decided to have one made-to-measure, but not in black or blue like the rest of the proletariat, mine would be silver grey. As I waited for the overcoat to arrive, I stocked up with the regulation accessories: real leather gloves, a silk paisley scarf and brand new shiny black brogues. The Crombie seemed to take an age to arrive, but finally the big day came, and it was a perfect fit. Boy, did I look the business. At lunchtime I decided to promenade down Piccadilly and Market Street to show off my stunning new look. Imagine the scene, light grey mohair suit, gleaming white shirt, old school style tie, the new Crombie, the new shiny black brogues, the silk paisley scarf and real leather gloves. My first stop was Dunn and Company, the hat makers, which was two doors down. I didn't want a hat, but I wanted the gorgeous girl who worked there to see my new look. I walked round the store for at least ten minutes, but not once did she look up from whatever she was doing. "Oh well, her loss," I thought, as I continued on my journey. I was hoping for lots of admiring glances and it's true to say that people were certainly looking at me, but for all the wrong reasons. What I had failed to take into account was that it was the middle of July, at least 80 degrees in the shade, and everybody else was wearing T-shirts and shorts. By the time I hit Market Street, the sweat was pouring off me. As I turned on my heel and began marching back, a bus stopped and a man got off and shouted: "Yeah, they said it might snow!" I steadfastly continued my march, but I could clearly hear a few stifled giggles. The reason I keep mentioning marching is because, at the time, I had developed this strange walk that, for some reason, I thought completed "the look". I would walk along the street swinging my right arm in the style of a Sergeant Major. The reason I developed this "Ministry of Silly Walks style"? You guessed it, Keith Hall did the exact same walk, but somehow, he could pull it off. One night, on my way home from "The Pop Inn" under-

18's disco, I caught the 53 bus home, marched up the stairs and marched to the back of the bus, right arm going ten to the dozen. I went past a group of older lads who, right on cue, started singing "Arm Swinger" to the tune of Shirley Bassey's Goldfinger. I tried to make out that it was water off a duck's back, but it seemed that every time (and I do mean 'every time') I got on a bus in the future, those same lads would be on and the song "Arm Swinger" would start to ring out.

One day, Keith took me to one side and told me about "The Scam". Everybody was doing it, it was dead easy - a chance to make a few quid.

CHAPTER NINE: "Brass in Pocket", The Pretenders 1979 (Number One)

Me and Keith were alone in the kitchen one day when he decided that it was time to take me into his confidence about a little money-making scam that every member of the sales staff was in on, except me. I mentioned earlier that one of the ways to make a bit of commission was by selling a suit that had been made to measure for someone but had never been collected. These suits were stored separately away from the normal stock. The scam worked like this: you sold somebody a suit, then you went to the unclaimed made-to-measure rack and rooted through until you found one of the same price. Then you swapped labels and could claim your 50p commission. Fifty pence doesn't sound much these days, but when you are only earning just over a fiver a week it wasn't to be sniffed at. Back in the early 70s you could go out with a couple of quid in your pocket, have a few pints, a great night out and still come home with change, and when it came to the scam if everybody else is doing it - why not?

You might have thought that the milk-stealing fiasco would have put me off Blackpool for life, but, although I can't remember why, me and my mate Billy got a taste for weekends on the Golden Mile. I had first met Bill when we were both 14 and he came to play for the all-conquering Bradford Athletic, formerly known as Denlaw FC. Bill was a cultured centre half and I fancied myself as a bit of a goal machine up front. Indeed, Bill was made captain of the team until one day he was caught by Mr Mason eating a bag of chips before a game. Me and Bill were inseparable for a few years and got into all sorts of scrapes. One night we had been to a mutual friend's birthday party and been hitting the whisky. Walking home, we first of all entertained the sleeping neighbourhood with a rousing sing-song then decided on a game of hopscotch in one or two household gardens. Of course, someone quite rightly called the police, we were chucked in the Black Maria and were summoned to court. Bill pleaded guilty and was given a caution but, because I considered that Bill was far more drunk than I was, I decided to plead not guilty and was fined ten pounds, which was more than a week's wages back in the day. On one of our first weekends in Blackpool we missed the last bus home on the Sunday night, had no money left and nowhere to stay. That particular afternoon we had played a couple of games of bingo and won - we both enjoyed a cheeky game of housey-housey back in those days - we hadn't bothered to claim our prizes but now decided that they might come in handy. We got back to the bingo stall just as they were closing for the night and hardly anybody was about. So I got on Bill's shoulders and helped myself to a handful of prizes. We didn't consider it stealing, we were just taking what was ours. Then we walked down the Golden Mile trying to sell them in order to get some money for digs for the night. We got talking to two Scottish girls who happened to mention that they could do with a kettle for their flat. Those lassies turned out to be very accommodating indeed.

The undisputed highlight of our weekends in Blackpool were Saturday nights at the 007 Club owned by former boxer Brian London. Brian was a flat-nosed hard-as-nails pugilist nicknamed "The Blackpool Rock" who had fought and lost to everyone, including Henry Cooper, Joe Bugner and the great Muhammed Ali. To be fair, he didn't actually fight Ali, rather than run away for three rounds until the greatest finally caught him, but fair play to Brian for getting in the ring in the first place. Brian was always on the door of the 007 Club looking mean and moody and you always held your breath when walking past him, just in case he took a dislike to you and wouldn't let you in. Once you were inside, the 007 was a fantastic night spot. Me and Bill would always go upstairs in the quiet lounge for a steak sandwich, which to this day remains the very best steak sandwich I have ever tasted. Chris Montez' greatest hits would always be playing in the background and inspired my lifelong love of a man I call "the greatest singer who couldn't sing a note". Have a listen to his 1966 hit "The More I See You" and you'll know what I mean. Having filled our faces and enjoyed a couple of 'liveners' it was time to go downstairs where all the action was taking place.

The prettiest girls in town could always be seen at the 007 Club. Sadly, so could the best-looking blokes, along with several members of the Blackpool football team, so me and Bill never stood a chance of copping off. However, the music was first class. The first time I heard the brilliant Northern Soul classic "At the Top of The Stairs" by the Formations was in the 007 and I've loved it ever since. The atmosphere was electric and thanks to Brian London there was never a hint of trouble. I did say we never copped off, but in fact, one night I did come close. Towards the end of the evening we both found ourselves dancing with a couple of girls, and we couldn't believe our luck. Then the lights went down and the smoochy last chance dance came on. I took this girl in my arms and stumbled round the dance floor cheek to cheek, occasionally exchanging knowing glances with Bill who was wrapped around his new girlie. Suddenly my nose started running and I thought to myself, "Oh, don't say you're coming down with a cold? Not now, please." All the way through the dance I was sniffing up, thinking that this was not giving a good impression. Finally, the music stopped, the lights went on, we both took a step back and to my horror the girl was covered in blood - I'd had a nose bleed all over the poor girl. I had not had a nose bleed in years, so why now? It must have been the excitement and the tension of copping off. The girl screamed and ran to the toilets, followed, of course, by her friend. Bill wasn't best pleased - and I was devastated. This regular sodding-off to Blackpool routine was proving a bit expensive so I decided I needed another moneymaking scam. As I mentioned earlier, almost every customer at Burton's paid in cash at the time, so on a Saturday when we were run off our feet if somebody gave me exactly the right money, I would slip it into my pocket and hope they didn't ask for a receipt, and they never did. I'm certainly not proud of stealing money but I justified it by telling myself that Montague Burton was ripping me off by paying me such ludicrously low wages in the first place.

One night me and Bill were in the queue for the all-night bus in Manchester city centre following a night out at the Explosion night club, which was the in-place to be seen at the time. The disc jockey was a real cool guy called Greg Edwards, who was a master of the turntable and would later present a few shows on Radio One. Greg and I would be reunited nearly 20 years later when he started working at Sunset Radio in Manchester, but back then all I could do is stare in admiration at a guy who was totally in control of his audience. Anyway, we got talking to a couple of girls called Penny and Sue, Bill made a bee line for the flamboyant Penny and I kind of got stuck with Sue. We went out as a foursome for a while, but nothing was ever going to happen with Sue. On the other hand, Bill was absolutely smitten by Penny and almost right away they became a serious item.

Meanwhile, back at Burton's things carried on as normal. I was still supplementing my meagre income to the tune of a few quid a week, just like most of the other members of staff, and certainly the younger ones. Then, one Monday morning, it all went pear-shaped when the auditors moved in to check the books. As a result, a few months later most of us were transferred to other branches. I was sent to Deansgate about half a mile away, which was no great upheaval and would lead to the unexpected re-awakening of my schoolboy disc jockey ambitions.

One of my new colleagues at the Deansgate branch of Burton's the Tailors was a lad about the same age as me called Malcolm, who turned out to have a part-time job as a disc jockey for local Manchester personality Ray Teret. Ray operated the Disco Express, which provided DJs for clubs in the North West and Midlands. He was a larger than life character who was always in the local paper with some publicity stunt or other. For instance, he was the first man in Manchester to wear hot pants, and I daresay the last. Ray was a protege of Jimmy Savile and had a lot of the same mannerisms. His association with Savile would come back to haunt him a few years ago, when he was imprisoned for 25 years, having been found guilty of having sex with underage girls back in the 70s.

Anyway, Malcolm would be forever racing off after work to dee-jay at such places as the Bird Cage in Ashton-under-Lyne, the Ritz in Manchesters city centre or the Blue Room in Sale, Cheshire. Suddenly my life seemed mindlessly dull by comparison and I started asking Malc if I could tag along to one of his gigs, and he kindly agreed. I say 'kindly', but he did have ulterior motives, because it meant he could leave me to play the records for the first half hour while he chatted up the girls as they wandered in. This was when I first realised that if you were the dee-jay, the girls approached you. No working up the courage to say 'hello' or to ask them to dance, because they did all the work - what an eye-opener for a diffident young no-hoper like me. One night in the Bird Cage, so called because the dee-jay booth looked just like a budgie's cage set in the middle of the dance floor, Ray Teret himself approached me and asked if I'd like to learn the ropes. I would be the warm-up guy for the main man. It was a three-month trial with no pay, but after I'd proved myself the 'sky was the limit' (Ray's words, not mine) and this music to my ears. I was now on the first rung of the dee-jay ladder - next stop Radio One.

For the next few months I was working till six o'clock at Burton's, rushing home to wolf my tea down, then straight out to some night club somewhere. Usually a big old-fashioned Mecca venue or a church hall that Teret had rented out to put on an under-18's disco. Not much of a showbiz lifestyle, admittedly, but I loved it and I threw myself into it with real enthusiasm. All my spare money was going on building up a record collection. My mum, as usual, was less than impressed. "Haven't you got enough records by now?" she would ask. I never failed to see how she could not understand thc ridiculousness of that statement.

After my three-month training period, Ray announced that I was now officially "on the team" and I would now be on wages. The princely sum of two quid a night. As well as keeping up the day job at Burton's I would be dee-jaying six nights a week:

Monday - the Ritz in Manchester
Wednesday - either Tiffany's in Rochdale or The Place in Stoke-on-Trent
Thursday - Tiffany's in Manchester
Friday and Saturday - the Piccadilly Club in Manchester
Sunday - Tiffany's in Rochdale

Quite often I would be getting home just as the milkman was delivering his daily pinta, then it was a quick couple of hours in bed and back to Burton's. Clearly something had to give.

Ray Teret had a pretty one-dimensional idea when it came to giving his dee-jays 'stage names'. My Burton's colleague Malcolm Dixon was christened "Mad Malc" although a more sensible straight-laced young lad you'd be hard pressed to meet. A lad called Sammy was given the name "Super Sammy". Meanwhile, I would now be known as "Jumpin' Johnny". For some reason, I was also given a bowler hat to wear. None of this bothered me, I was just happy to find myself being paid to play records.

I was normally teamed up with Ray's right-hand man Mel Scholes and, as it turned out, there would be no better teacher. Mel could really work an audience, that's if you could persuade him to drag himself away from the bar and actually get on stage. One night we had just finished a gig at Tiffany's in Manchester when we decided to nip into the all-night greasy spoon cafe next door for a cuppa and a bacon sarnie. We sat near the window and began tucking in, when we became aware of a young down-and-out tapping on the window begging for a cup of tea. This poor wretch was only about 20-years-old, and, at the time, it was unusual to actually come into contact with somebody sleeping rough. If you go into Manchester these days, you can barely move for people dossing down on street corners and in shop doorways. In fact, the last time I went into Manchester, I found it desperately sad, as well as being scary and intimidating. "Cup o' tea, please, just a cup o' tea," the young man repeated, over and over again. Eventually, Mel said: "Johnny, for God's sake, get this bloke a cup of tea, he's driving me mad." I took the tea out to the freezing cold lad and said: "There you go mate, a nice hot cup of tea." The young man looked at me, looked at the cup and said: "Is there any sugar in it?" I assured him that, yes, there were two sugars in the tea. Without pausing, he said: "I only take one and half!"

Saturdays were spent at the Cat's Whiskers in Burnley, a big old cabaret-style venue that was always packed. I would do the dee-jaying while Mel was the host, entertaining the audience with a few gags before introducing the "special guest star", usually a comedian or singer. The Cat's Whiskers also had a resident band, Ted Poole and the Aristocats, who would bang out their half-decent versions of the hits of the day. I was never sure why they were needed because the punters would definitely prefer to dance to the real thing, as provided by me on record. I loved working at the Cat, but we had to leave town quite suddenly when Mel became aware that Ted Poole had paid a couple of local headcases to give him a good hiding. Apparently, Mel had become a little too close to the band's lead singer, Mrs Ted Poole. I would be reunited with Mel nearly 30 years later at Signal Radio, by which time he had established himself as a true local legend. When he died the amount of people who attended his funeral was quite phenomenal, it really was like the passing of a much-loved superstar, maybe a Bruce Forsyth or Eric Morecambe. I was asked to read his favourite poem and how I got through it I'll never know. I was genuinely shaking like a leaf. It's the old 'appearing in front of people' thing again.

But things at home were about to take a devastating turn for the worse and lead me, my mother and, most of all, my father into a dark period of madness. Our world was about to come crashing down round our ears. Nothing could have prepared us for what followed during the next couple of years.

One day I walked into the house to find my dad with his shoe and sock off showing mum a little innocuous-looking red spot just above his ankle. It was irritating rather than painful, but showing no sign of going away, so Dad very reluctantly made an appointment with the doctor. Dad never went to the doctors: "Bloody quacks, the lot of them," was his considered opinion, an opinion shared, I think, by a lot of his generation. However, the doc was concerned and booked the old man in for tests. The doctor came straight to the point: Dad's lungs were the same colour as his nicotine-stained fingers, so he would have to give up smoking immediately. Well, Dad certainly wasn't having that, he worked bloody hard and at the end of the day, if he couldn't have a pint and a Woodbine, what was the point? In truth, you never saw my dad without a fag in his hand, I never bothered counting just how many he got through in a day, but he always seemed to be sending me to the corner shop for "ten Woodies and a box of Swan Vestas". Over the next few months the tiny spot got bigger and more porous. The doctor didn't mince his words, years of smoking had hardened the arteries and Dad was in serious danger of losing his leg. He was immediately transferred to Buxton Hospital. Now, I assume Buxton Hospital was a place where they specialised in such problems, because they couldn't have chosen a more difficult place to get to. Every single day for months my mum juggled her full-time job in the cafeteria at British Home Stores in the centre of Manchester with the four-bus journey there and back to Buxton. I really was selfishly ignorant of the incredible stress she was under at this time - as long as my breakfast, dinner and tea were on the table, I assumed she was coping fine, as she always did. This went on for what must have been 18 months until one night my shattered-looking mum walked through the door with my dad limping behind her. This was the start of the most trying time in all our lives. The doctors had told dad that his leg would have to come off, and Dad's reaction was swift and to the point. He told them to "Eff Off" and discharged himself. Being hospitalised, he had been forced to stop boozing and, with all the medication he was taking, this amazingly did not seem to bother him, but he could never give up Woodbines. Looking back, the old feller must have been in agony and no doubt fearful of what the future held and it certainly didn't make him easy to live with. He was in a filthy mood every waking minute and quite often seemed to be hallucinating. He accused the club man of chatting up my mum when the poor chap had simply turned up to collect his weekly ten bob, or whatever it was. "Piss off out of my house, you effing Gigolo," he screamed. Dad was like a lot of his peers, largely self-educated and he pronounced 'gigolo' as in gig – 'giggolo'. To be fair, the hapless club man could not have looked less like a gigolo if he'd tried, with his checkered car coat and his light brown Hush Puppies, he looked more like Harry Worth than Sacha Distel. My poor old mother was at her wit's end and finally accepted my Auntie Angie's invitation to move in with her for a few days' peace and quiet. I really couldn't blame her, but this meant I was alone in the house with my increasingly barking mad dad. He got it into his muddled, medicated head that mum had not gone to Angie's at all but had run off with "that bastard Giggolo". Around this time, he got into the habit of phoning the police, firstly to tell them that his wife had left him to fend for himself and had set up home with a 'giggolo'. No matter how many times I reminded him that the word was pronounced 'gigolo', he just didn't seem to take it in. The police, needless to say, were not too impressed with the call, and they were equally unimpressed when he phoned the cop shop to inform them that I had left the house without putting any coal on the fire. In fact, I hadn't left the house at all, I was getting ready to go to out when he had asked me to put some coal on the fire, and I replied, "In a minute," and went upstairs. This was enough to set him off again. Two detectives did call round when dad phoned to say a murderer was living in the same road. At the time the police were searching frantically for the Black Panther who had kidnapped and murdered Staffordshire heiress Lesley Whittle, and my dad had become absolutely unshakably convinced that the Black Panther was, in fact, Keith who lived next door but one and played darts in the local boozer. The officers managed to keep straight faces as they dutifully took note of all my dad's suspicions. He also convinced himself that he had been treated shabbily by the doctors at Buxton Hospital, and began writing long, detailed, but incomprehensible letters to whoever he imagined might listen. He wrote to the Daily Express, the Daily Mirror, the Daily Mail, even the communist paper the Daily Star. He wrote to Granada and the BBC and then to Harold Wilson. "He won't sweep it under the carpet, he'll make sure he gets to the bottom of it," he said, convincing nobody but himself. Whatever there was to investigate, nobody seemed the slightest bit interested, as there were never any replies. It was usually my job to post these letters, but when he sent me to the post box with letters addressed to the National Front and Gay News, I decided it was time to file them - in the bin.

On Sunday the 7th of July 1974, I had just settled down to watch the World Cup Final between West Germany and the exciting total footballers of Holland when there was a knock at the door. It was our local Member of Parliament who, armed with a handful of dad's old letters, had decided he had better come and see the old fool. At last somebody was at least showing some kind of interest. The MP spent the whole of the World Cup Final listening to my dad's complaints before leaving the house, never to be heard from again.

After a few days, my mum came home and Dad seemed to calm down for a while, but he was soon back to his demented old self. Dad was certainly suffering, he was certainly in agony, but it was also hell on Earth for me and my long-suffering mum.

It was about eight o'clock on a Sunday morning when I heard my mum talking to our next-door neighbour. Mum was in floods of tears and, listening carefully, I was soon able to put two and two together - Dad had suffered a heart attack in the night and was dead. I'm ashamed to say that my initial reaction was one of relief. I spent the rest of that Sunday driving round to relatives informing them of the bad news and it wasn't till much later that what had happened really hit me and I burst into tears. Dad was 49 years old.

One morning, I turned up for work at Burton's as usual, half asleep and 20 minutes late, when the manager called me into his office and issued an ultimatum. This could not go on any longer, I would have to choose between a career in retailing or playing records for a living. I thought long and hard (about ten seconds, actually) before deciding I was now a professional disc jockey. But what on Earth was my mum going to say?

Another phone call that Dad had made to the police had serious consequences for me. More of that later. By this time, I had passed my driving test and, although I eventually passed first time, I spent a fortune on driving lessons and must have gone through at least half a dozen different instructors. Reversing was my biggest problem, and I still can't fully get the hang of it to this day. My first instructor was a bit of a chancer from the British School of Motoring. He would start the lesson by telling me what a mess his life was and end it by tapping me up for a couple of quid, which I never got back. Other blokes would take me out for one lesson, promise to return the next week, only to be never seen again, their nerves presumably in tatters.

By now, I was still working regularly for Ray Teret but his "empire" was starting to crumble - he had lost all his Mecca Venues and was reduced to hiring various Town Halls to put on under-18's disco nights, which were usually poorly-attended. I had started going out with a really nice girl called

Val, who also worked for Ray on a part-time basis as a box office cashier in one or two of his weekly town hall discos. Her proper job was a nursery nurse and, in truth, she was a bit of a blonde bombshell and I couldn't believe my luck. Val's Mum, Olive, was a hairdresser, who ran her own business from a salon in West Didsbury, an up-market area of Manchester, a mile or so from where I lived in the decidedly less salubrious Withington. Val's family lived in the flat above the salon. Olive was a young at heart 50-something who, every weekend, hit the town with her much younger toy boy Terry, who was about a year older than me. Terry was the manager of the local cinema, so I was double quids-in: free haircuts from Olive and free cinema tickets from Terry. It was Olive who gave me my Marc Bolan perm that I loved, but once again it didn't go down too well at home. Mum said I looked like a big girl's blouse and for once my dad was a little more subtle: "Started bowling from the pavilion end, have we, son?" - a phrase that, even back then, made me giggle. And, thanks to Terry, me and Val were able to see all the big films of the day without once putting my hand in my pocket. Her Dad was Reg, the man from the Prudential by day, and part-time bouncer for Ray Teret by night. Reg was a gruff old boy and always seemed to be in a bad mood and I could never understand why he so meekly put up with Olive and her toy boy. Maybe he was just glad of the peace and quiet. Val had a younger brother Nigel who was about 16 and had just left school to work for the gas board. Nigel was a decent enough lad, very effeminate and obviously gay, although none of the family thought to mention it. After about a year, me and Val kind of got fed up of each other and the relationship fizzled out. Perhaps I should have tried a bit harder because Nigel became Nigel Martin Smith who went on to put together the boy band Take That and became a multi-millionaire.

Reg was a bit of a car enthusiast and liked to go down to the second-hand car auctions at Belle Vue every week. Reg came up with the idea of me giving him £10 a week and, when it got to about a hundred pounds, he would get me a suitable car from the auction. As I knew absolutely bugger all about cars this seemed like a great idea. A week or so after I had passed my test, Reg turned up behind the wheel of what looked like a World War Two Tank. It was my new car, a hideous dark green Hillman Minx for which he had paid £90. I hated it. It was grotesque and definitely an old man's car. I pretended to be grateful while all the time thinking "my mates are going to have a field day. This car is a piss-take on a plate". And what was my Mum going to say, me turning up on the doorstep driving a green car? Mum hated the colour green and would never have it in the house, she was absolutely convinced that the colour green brought nothing but bad luck.

As it turned out, she didn't have too long to fret about my hideous green gas guzzler. After about two weeks I crashed it into a Transit van being driven by this enormous black bloke who, thankfully for me, found himself trapped, unable to open his driver's door. So, he was unable to perform any of the acts he was describing to me.

My second car was a Ford Anglia which cost me £45. When I handed over the cash, I failed to realise that the clutch was slipping and a week later car number two was consigned to the scrap yard. Car number three was a brown Ford Cortina. Soon after buying it I lost the keys but found that I could open the door and drive off using my front door Yale key. Not surprisingly, it was always being stolen and pretty soon I was on first name terms with the copper on the desk at Withington Police Station. "Not again?" he would say, as I rang the bell on his desk.

One night, I was driving home from the Locarno in Blackpool and I got as far as turning into my road when a police car came out of nowhere and pulled in front of me. They had reason to believe I had been drinking and would I be kind enough to blow into this bag? As it turned out, the weather had been atrocious that day and, as a result, the Locarno had been virtually empty, so we closed early and Dave the Bar Manager invited me to have a night cap at a drinking club he frequented. Dave was a really nice guy and we got on very well - up until recently, he had worked as a roadie for Smokie and, before that, the Faces. That very night he told me a story about Rod Stewart which, to this day, I'm still not sure whether to believe or not, but seeing as Rod is quite litigious, I won't repeat it. Anyway, we had a couple of pints and I went on my way. As I blew into the breathalyser, I was still quite relaxed because I felt stone cold sober, but the reading told a different story. I was just over the limit and was taken back to the police station for a blood test. That too was positive. Brilliant, just a few months after passing my test I was facing a big fine and a driving ban. The following morning Dad proudly revealed to me that *he* had phoned the police to tell them that I would be driving home from Blackpool and that I would have been drinking. Apparently, I had said or done something to annoy him before I left the house so he did his usual party piece of phoning the Old Bill.

It was Ray Teret who advised me to make an appointment with a particular solicitor who he said was the one person who might be able to get me off. This, of course, was the 70s when the attitude to being breathalysed was "There but for the grace of God".

The meeting with the solicitor was unremarkable, until I got up to leave and he casually asked me if anybody had laced my drinks on that fateful night. When I said "no", he said, "Are you sure? Ask around, because you never know." It didn't take Einstein to understand what he was getting at and it certainly planted a seed. As it turned out, my mate Dave from the Locarno was only too happy to come to court and swear on the bible that it was indeed he who had surreptitiously dropped a couple of vodkas in my lager, on the basis that he wanted to stay out drinking while I was determined to go home. Come the big day in court, Dave was word perfect and the magistrate believed us both. I was fined a tenner and my license endorsed, but no ban. We walked out of the court and straight into the pub next door for a celebratory pint.

CHAPTER TEN: "The Long and Winding Road", The Beatles (Album Track 1970)

Around this time, I was sending demo tapes to almost every radio station in the country but getting a steady stream of rejection letters. I wish I'd kept them, I think they might have made interesting reading. It was my ambition to get a job on my local commercial station, Piccadilly Radio, and I did get a couple of interviews with the legendary programme controller Colin Walters, but nerves got the better of me and I completely blew it. Colin was quite a scary individual and I became a garbling nincompoop every time I sat down in front of him. Looking back, some of the demo tapes I made were pretty good and sounded a lot better than some of the presenters already working on "Picc", but I could never do myself justice when it came to the interview. In fairness, I have always been rubbish at interviews, no matter how many times I rehearsed what I was going to say, the whole thing would turn to shite come the big day.

I was still earning a decent living in the clubs, however, and one day I heard on the grapevine that Pips nightclub were looking for a disc jockey, so I was on the phone straight away. Pips was the biggest disco in Manchester, and usually packed, and I'd always quite fancied working there. "Can you come down tomorrow night for an audition?" said the manager. I told him I was very experienced, and he must have heard of me (he hadn't) so I explained that I didn't do auditions, but I was quite prepared to work for a night and, if he didn't think I was any good, he didn't need to pay me.

This was a ploy I always used, and it always worked for me. So, I walked in for my first night, struggling as always with my record boxes, and I recognised the manager right away. The last time I had seen him he called the police and accused me of beating up his head doorman. I swallowed something hard and jagged and offered my hand. Thankfully he didn't recognise me.

Some three years earlier there had been a knock on the door. I was getting ready for a bath, so my mum opened the door. I heard this bloke saying he was from the police and he wanted to speak to John Owen. My heart sank, I was still working at Burton's at the time and I immediately assumed that my money-making scams had been rumbled. I went downstairs and when the police officer said he was investigating an assault on a night club doorman the relief was palpable. I tried to explain that it was nothing to do with me but then, just like on the telly, he said, "You're not obliged to say anything, but you are under arrest for grievous bodily harm." My mum's legs gave way and she fell onto the settee. The copper said I would have to "accompany" them to the station to sort it out. My mum wanted to come with me, but they said she couldn't, but don't worry, they wouldn't keep me long.

When I got to Bootle Street police station the full scale of the trouble I was in was explained to me. There had been an almighty battle outside the club one night and the head doorman, a 20-stone brute of a man, had been knocked to the ground, kicked in the head and was currently in Ancoats hospital.

As I stood at the desk waiting for whatever I was waiting for, there was a bloke next to me, obviously the worse for wear on either drink or drugs, mouthing off to the desk sergeant. When I looked at him properly my heart sank, it was a lad from school. I recognised him immediately as a troublemaker who was always in bother, I looked at him and he looked at me and I found myself thinking: "I'm in enough of a mess here, mate, please don't let on you know me." Thankfully, he was in such a state, nothing seemed to register.

I tried to explain to the two officers that I was not in the club on that particular night, I was in fact working for Ray Teret that night and if they would only phone Ray, he could confirm it. I realised I was in the middle of a good cop, bad cop scenario. One detective appeared friendly and reasonable, the other was just the opposite. "Ray Teret!" spat out the nasty one. "He's no good, I once arrested him for nicking a car." Now I really was getting worried. "I know you did this," continued Mr Nasty. "The girl on the box office recognised you straight away and so did the manager, you're bang to rights." Bang to rights? I have never understood what that means but it was definitely something Jack Regan might say, just after he'd said, "We're the Sweeney, son, and you're nicked."

I tried to explain that at five foot something and eight stone wet through I was hardly capable of beating up a 20-stone doorman or anyone else for that matter. "I haven't been involved in any kind of fight since I was in the school playground," I pleaded. "And even then, I lost."

Various policemen came walking past and I could see them looking at me and looking at the detectives as if to say "surely this can't be right" but Mr Nasty seemed determined to see me hung, drawn and quartered. After about an hour of this nonstop aggressive interrogation, I was almost starting to believe that I was guilty. The police definitely had me believing I was going to be locked up, for a long time.

Eventually, I was released at three o'clock in the morning on condition I attended an identity parade in a few days' time. The girl on the box office, who was sure I was responsible, would be trying to identify the culprit. This didn't fill me with confidence because me and my mate Bill would always take the mickey out of this girl for being so miserable whenever we were signing in. Hang on a minute - signing in! That was it, all the police had to do was check the signing in book on the night all this happened, and they would see right away that I hadn't been in the club that night. I put this enthusiastically to Inspector Nasty, but he disdainfully brushed it aside. This did not fit in with his scenario at all and he was having none of it. When I was eventually let go, I realised I had no money and would have to walk home.

When I arrived back at gone five o'clock my mum was wide awake and still on the settee. "I told you this dee-jaying lark would all end in tears," she said, helpfully.

After days of worry I turned up at the police station for the identity parade to be told by Inspector Nasty that Ray Teret had indeed verified that I was working for him on the night it had all kicked off and so I was free to go. "Tell me one thing before you go - did you do it?" he said. I was very polite, but I couldn't help thinking, "you pillock".

So here I was three years later a free man and about to start as the resident disc jockey at Manchester's number one venue.

I loved working at Pips, it was always busy and at weekends coach loads of people would turn up from all parts of the country. The club had four rooms, including the Funk Room, which specialised in underground American dance music. It seemed to me that the only time people actually went in there was when all the other dance floors were too full to get on. There was the Soul Room, which was the domain of Mike Shaft who, by night, was a cool black guy in a white hat who had taken the name of an American detective made famous in a popular film of the same name. By day he was a post office cashier, but many years later he would give me a much-needed leg-up in the world of radio, and I owe a hell of a lot to Mike Shaft. Mike is still working today, presenting the Sunday morning show on BBC Radio Manchester, having been the basketball commentator for Sky Sports in the mid-90s. There was the Roxy Room, dominated by weird-looking creatures of the night, dolled up to look like either David Bowie, Bryan Ferry or various members of the New York Dolls. Smack in the middle was me, in the Chart Room, which meant I got to play everything that was worth playing in the charts, including funk and soul hits and any Bowie or Roxy Music records that were in the Top 40. Basically, I was playing the music everybody wanted to hear, so my room was always bursting at the seams, it was great fun.

The only fly in the ointment was the fact that the owner, Gerald Summers, a local tycoon with carefully bouffant hair and an eye for the young ladies, hated alcohol and his number one rule was no drinking on duty. Now, I've always needed a bit of Dutch courage to speak down the mic in front of an audience, so you always had to keep one eye on the whereabouts of the management as you had a glug of your secret pint hidden in the DJ booth. In a darkened radio studio talking to myself, I'm in my element, but coming face-to-face with the public is quite another matter. Many years later when I was established on the radio, I was booked to do a series of personal appearances at a huge Manchester disco. The idea of standing in front of an audience as the "star turn" terrified me so much I found myself throwing up in the toilet, so I had to turn my back on that very nice little earner.

One particular Friday night, my old banger had refused to start so I had to get a taxi which, as far as I was concerned, meant that I was free to imbibe a bit more than usual. And why stick to lager when the rocket fuel also known as Carlsberg Special was available. Come one o'clock in the morning, I was gloriously under the influence and decided to play the new David Essex song and nothing else for the last hour. So, from one o'clock until chucking-out time, the lucky punters were treated to Hold Me Close non-stop with me singing along down the microphone at the top of my voice. "Hold me close don't let me go, oh no."

Although the following night I had a bit of explaining to do, that last hour went down in legend within the Manchester DJ fraternity and would go a long way to getting me a job at what was officially the Best Disco in Britain. More of that later.

Like I say, Pips was the biggest disco in Manchester, possibly the whole country, it was advertised on the telly and coaches would come from all over the place. One Saturday night in December a girl came over to the DJ booth to ask for a record. She was quite attractive and, of course, having enjoyed a couple of pints I started chatting her up and arranged to give her a lift home. At the end of the night she was still waiting, so I thought "You've cracked it, Johnny Boy" and we made our way to my car which, at the time, was a bright yellow Mini. Even though it was a freezing cold night, all I was wearing was a Hawaiian short-sleeved shirt and a pair of white cotton flares - standard attire for DJs at the time. We got in the car and I asked her where she lived. "Todmorden" was the reply. I had never heard of the place. It seems she had come by coach but had told her mates that she had "pulled the DJ" and he was giving her a lift home. She informed me that to get to Todmorden you had to leave Manchester, go through Oldham and when you get up to Rochdale you just keep going. I eventually realised that to get to Todmorden you have to keep going and going till you can't go any further. then you keep going some more. As we finally entered Todmorden at something like half past three in the morning, it had started snowing and was coming down pretty heavily. "It snows all the time round here," said my new lady friend. When we finally got to her house, she told me we couldn't go in, but there was a school just around the corner and the gates were always open. Well, I thought, I've come all this way, in for a penny, in for a pound. By this time, the snow was really coming down and the dodgy windscreen wipers on my old Mini were not up to the job and I could barely see a thing. As I drove round the school playground looking for a discreet place to do our "courting" I noticed a set of cricket stumps. As I tried to drive round the wickets…BANG…the stumps had been painted on the wall and I had driven head first into it. I swear, Van Gogh must have painted those cricket stumps, they were so realistic! What a passion killer, I drove the girl back to her house gave her a peck on the cheek, she got out, slammed the door and stormed indoors.

As I started to head home through the black hills of Todmorden, smoke began emanating from the engine, and the car came to an abrupt halt. Here I was miles and miles from home, it was snowing like nobody's business, and here's me in my short-sleeved shirt and white cotton flares, freezing cold. As I climbed into the cramped back seat to try and get my head down, I mulled over the fact that it had not been a great night. Spent a fortune in petrol, the car was dead, I was sure I would die of hypothermia before dawn and not the slightest hint of a leg over!

It was just about this time that Bill announced that he and Penny were getting married. I was first of all amazed that they had made a go of it because, while Bill was like me, fairly shy and reserved, Penny was a real extrovert in both looks and personality. I was, of course, delighted for my old mate, and started to prepare for my best man duties. There was a speech that needed writing and I also called in to my old Burton's branch on Piccadilly to be measured for a brand new bespoke three-piece suit, I needed to look the part, couldn't let the side down. However, as the weeks went by towards the big day, it began to dawn on me that Bill had made no mention of me being best man and I soon learned that I had been overlooked in favour of one of his workmates. I was hurt and devastated, how could this happen? After all we had been through on the football field over the years and our escapades in Blackpool. It's true to say that we were no longer as close as we had been, but I had been busy trying to carve out a new career and if the situation had been reversed Bill would still have been my automatic choice. There was no scene, no argument and no big bust-up, I simply stopped talking to him. To my eternal shame, it would stay that way for nearly 40 years. What a stupid way to end a great friendship. Sorry, Bill, what can I say? I behaved like an idiot. Incidentally, I never did collect that made-to-measure whistle from Burton's, I dare say some lucky sod was able to make a 50p bonus when he eventually found somebody who it fitted.

One Sunday afternoon in 1976, myself and a few other DJs were invited by a record company to go to Liverpool for a meet and greet with Jimmy James and The Vagabonds. A free glass of wine, a few nibbles and the chance to talk to Jimmy, who was in the charts at the time with a great disco record called "Now is the Time". Jimmy was great company and it was a terrific afternoon, but as I made my way home down the motorway, my newly acquired 12-year-old Volkswagen Beetle huffed and puffed and finally died. Apparently, you have to put oil and water in your car from time to time, who knew? I felt especially guilty because I had bought the car for £100 from an elderly couple who only agreed to sell me the car on the understanding that I would look after it as well as they had done. Although the car was old it was in pristine condition. I genuinely felt that I had let the really nice old couple down. But the Beetle could not be brought back to life and I would have to fork out for another car. Apart from dropping really lucky with the Beetle, I had a series of cheap old bangers in the 70s that were definitely more trouble than they were worth. You could just about get away with it in the 1970s because most people drove an old banger. I also owned a clapped-out old rust bucket of a Mini (not the Todmorden one) that was a magnet for the Old Bill. One night, I was stopped because the indicators weren't working, and as the police officer stared at the car in disbelief, I mumbled something about planning to part exchange it the next week. "Exchange it for what?" asked the officer. "A fucking pogo stick!"

I did say that my first car was a Hillman Minx, but actually, I tell a lie. The Hillman Minx was my second car. My first was a Triumph Herald bought after just one driving lesson from a DJ mate of mine called Roger Willans for a tenner. This was another lad who worked for Ray Teret. Now Teret, as I mentioned earlier, had a thing for naff nicknames, but when Roger joined "the firm" Teret was at a loss. 'Roger the Rogerer' certainly didn't work, and 'Roger the Dodger' was too naff even for a Ray Teret protege. So, I came up with 'Roger the Artful' as in the Artful Dodger. Roger was delighted and still uses it to this day for his mobile disco gigs. Another moniker I came up with that I was proud of was given to a lad who while dee-jaying would put on various hats and do impressions. For instance, he would put on a fez and do Tommy Cooper or a cowboy hat and do a quick John Wayne. After careful deliberation I gave him the name "Maddie The Hat", mad as a hatter, get it?

Anyway, back to Roger the Artful's Triumph Herald. After just one fairly disastrous driving lesson, I decided to invest a tenner in this barely held together death trap, and on the Saturday afternoon I had the bright idea of taking it for a quick spin round the block. I got around the corner and had to stop because I could not find second gear. When I re-started the thing, it shot across the road and crashed head-on into a garden wall. The woman of the house opened the door, looked at the carnage and disappeared inside again. I got out of the car and followed her into the house, by which time she was dialling a number that I assumed was the police. Panic-stricken, I took the phone out of her hand and slammed it down. "Please don't call the police," I pleaded, "I'll pay for any damage." After threatening to skin me alive, my mum, bless her, paid a brickie to sort it out and I never heard anything more. Mum had to move quickly and quietly before the old man got wind of it.

On my night off I used to love going down to another Manchester night club called the Cellar Vie Wine Bar. My best mate at the time, a lad called Steve, was the resident DJ, and it was always a cracking night out. One night, Kathy Dooley, the lead singer of The Dooleys pop group, was in the club with a couple of friends and once again I'd enjoyed a few glasses of falling-down water. I bumped into Kathy at the bar and said: "I've just bought one of your records." She asked which one, so right on cue I replied "I've Got You by The Dooleys". Amazingly, she started to laugh, so I thought I would chance my arm even further by asking her to dance. So, there I was dancing with Kathy Dooley. Now, at the time The Dooley's were one of the most popular groups in Britain having enjoyed a whole string of hit records, indeed only a few nights earlier Kathy had been on Top of The Pops with the rest of the group belting out their latest top five song. So, in my giddy, alcohol-imbued haze, I started to think that I needed to do something that would impress this superstar. I have no idea how or why I came up with what I did next but even writing it down now I am filled with self-loathing. I decided to impress Kathy by doing the "Batusi" or Batdance, a 1960s go-go dance invented for the Batman TV series, as demonstrated by Adam West as the Caped Crusader on telly some years earlier. I know, I know, the worst idea anybody has ever had, but at the time... The dance involves making a horizontal V-sign with your index and middle fingers before drawing them across the front of the eyes, away from the centre of the face simultaneously, in time with the music. What could possibly go wrong? Anyway, Kathy suddenly declared that she had to go to the ladies and, guess what, she never came back. One morning a letter came through the door completely out of the blue. It was from BBC Radio Manchester and my heart skipped a couple of beats. Radio Manchester was one of the stations that I had sent demo tapes to and, like all the others, I still had the rejection letters, but why on earth were they writing to me now? Perhaps they had seen the error of their ways and now they couldn't wait to offer me a show. Radio Manchester was the staid and unambitious local BBC station that hardly anybody listened to, certainly me and my mates would never consider giving it the time of day. It had always been a bit fuddy-duddy, and since Piccadilly Radio had sparkled into life some twelve months earlier, it had virtually disappeared from people's radars. Still, it was a radio station and they had written to me and not the other way around, so I ripped the envelope open with excited anticipation. They were planning a new radio talent show called "New Voices" and they wanted me to be on it. The letter invited me to a meeting with the station manager Derek Woodcock.

I got to the Radio Manchester building in plenty of time, unlike my first day at Burton's, and was advised to take the lift to Mr Woodcock's office. I can't begin to describe how nervous I was as I waited for that lift. After all, this really was the chance of a lifetime. Eventually the lift came down, the doors opened, and two men got out. The first thing I noticed was that one of the men was wearing pink shoes, then I noticed his blue satin jacket, then his explosion of curly hair. I assumed he must be another DJ, another would-be contestant, who had also been summoned to see Mr Woodcock. As we passed each other we made eye contact, nodded, and both said "all right" almost under our breath, like you do with strangers, but as the doors shut and the lift started to rise I suddenly realised - it was Marc Bolan, one of my great musical heroes and the man that, a few years later, my son would be named after.

I had just come face-to-face with the one and only Marc Bolan and all I could manage to mumble was a feeble "all right". Who could have guessed that just two years later this gorgeous creature, and he was a fantastic-looking bloke, would be dead at just 29 years of age? The first thing I spluttered to the very conservatively dressed Derek Woodcock was "I've just seen Marc Bolan". Derek seemed underwhelmed: "Oh, yes, I believe he was in today." I supposed that someone like the manager of a radio station must see famous people all the time.

At the meeting Derek explained that "New Voices" was inspired by the hit TV series "New Faces" which in the mid-70s was must-see Saturday night viewing, the "Britain's Got Talent" of its day, and the show which introduced the country to some prestigious future superstars including Victoria Wood, Les Dennis, Michael Barrymore and a very young Lenny Henry, who brought the house down when he came on stage, back to the camera, and started doing the obligatory (at the time) impression of Frank Spencer, the punchline being, of course, that Lenny was black. The show also featured an unknown rock n roll band from the Midlands called Showaddywaddy (more of them later). Derek explained that his version would feature people who were desperate to break into radio, 13 hopefuls would be included and each one would be given one hour, starting at 10pm on a Friday night, to show what they could do, and Derek, alongside a team of producers, would choose a winner, who would be given a six-week contract to present a weekly show. I was pencilled in as number nine on the list. "Was I interested?" asked Derek. I thought about it for all of a split-second before snapping his hand off. One of my competitors and the person chosen to do the first show was a university professor who called himself Julius K. Scragg. I knew Julius vaguely because he also dabbled as a part time disc jockey on the Manchester club scene. He was a bedraggled eccentric hippy type, who loved to use phrases like "peace, love and understanding". He looked a bit like the TV Wizard Catweazle, but he was also fiercely determined to get into radio. There was also a fair few people taking part who would go on to have excellent careers in radio, including Gary Davies (that's the one, Ooooh, Gary Davies) who would a few years later host the lunchtime show on the mighty (at the time) Radio One. There was Mark Jones, who would have a long and successful association with Radio City in Liverpool, plus one or two others, but I still felt that Catweazle was the man to beat. I listened intently to Julius's show and it was very good, but I wasn't too impressed with any of the others. Finally came week nine and my chance to show what I could do. I hardly slept a wink in the days before the show and on the Friday itself I was shaking with nerves. I see young would-be presenters these days and they seem to be confident, assured and often cocky – well, those three words certainly could not be applied to how I was feeling. I got into the studio at 9.30pm and was introduced to the on-air presenter who called himself "The Baron". He was Radio Manchester's best-known presenter and he did nothing to calm my nerves, just the opposite in fact. He swivelled in his chair, choosing the next record while juggling with his jingle carts and talking to a listener on the phone. I sat in the corner, open-mouthed, sweating like a pig waiting for the abattoir van to turn up. When his show finished and the news started, The Baron sat in his swivel chair talking on the phone for as long as he could, leaving me hardly any time to make myself comfortable and remind myself how everything worked. When I finally sat down and looked at the desk my mind went totally blank. Which knob worked what? Which fader faded what? Suddenly, the news finished, and I was on. 'Don't mess this up, Johnny Boy, or you'll regret it for the rest of your miserable life'. This was a time when every presenter still had their own theme tune, and I had chosen an instrumental called "Get Lost Jack Frost" by John Barry. Listening to it now, it sounds really old-fashioned, but at the time I thought it was quite catchy. On reflection it sounds a bit like "When the Saints Go Marching In" and if you want to check it out you can find it on You Tube (along with the Batusi dance). The idea is, you play a bit of your theme tune then burst on the air with some kind of snappy introduction, I put the fader up and went to say something, but then bottled out and put it down again. This happened three or four times before the producer spoke down the talk-back and said, "I think you'd better say something".

I took a very deep breath and went for it. "Good evening, Radio Manchester, my name is Johnny Owen, I don't know why but there it is (why I decided to do a Harry Worth impression at this time, I will really never know, but I continued). "I am number nine on the list of 13 potential New Voices and, by the way, that commotion you can hear in the background is the great Lord Reith spinning in his grave. I'm sure when he founded the British Broadcasting Corporation all those years ago this is exactly what he had in mind: a scruffy uneducated urchin from the slums of Bradford introducing Elton John singing Philadelphia Freedom." I chose Elton John to start the show, not because it was one of my favourites, but because it was nearly six minutes long. Time to relax a bit and get my breath back. I followed Elton with Duane Eddy's big hit of the day "Play Me Like You Play Your Guitar". After my stuttering start, suddenly there was no stopping me, this is what I was born to do and, amazingly, I was bloody good at it. I had arranged to have the night off from Pips so when the show finished, I went to see my mate Steve at The Cellar Vie wine bar and got very pleasantly sozzled. I spent the night half-expecting someone to come up to me and say "Didn't I hear you on Radio Manchester earlier, you were brilliant." Sadly, no one did.

The New Voices series came to an end and, about two weeks later on a Saturday morning, having heard nothing from the Beeb, I was still in bed having worked at Pips the night before when my mum came into my bedroom looking flustered. "There's a couple of beatniks at the door and they're asking for you," she said. A brief description of the said "beatniks" convinced me that one of them was Julius K. Scragg. I asked my mum to make them a brew and I'd be right down. She was back upstairs in no time and said, "They want to take tea on the lawn." Describing our postage stamp of a front garden as a lawn was a mighty leap of the imagination, but a sneaky peak out of the bedroom window confirmed that it was indeed Julius and a woman I'd never seen before, but who I would soon discover was Mrs Scragg. They were both sitting cross legged like Red Indians getting ready for a pow-pow, and she was bare footed. I quickly dressed and went outside to be greeted by a foul tempered Julius who said: "You Bastard!" "What?" I replied. "You absolute bastard, you've won!"

It turned out that Julius had grabbed the bull by the horns and rang Derek Woodcock to find out when the announcement would be made that he was the "New Voices" champion and when he was going to start his six-week stint, only to be told that, in fact, I had got the most votes. I duly got a call from Mr Woodcock and arrangements were made for me to begin my series of shows in a few weeks' time. Needless to say, I was absolutely made up, this was surely the best day of my life.

In the meantime, I got on with dee-jaying at Pips. Every Saturday a presenter from Piccadilly Radio would turn up to do a personal appearance and I would give up the DJ booth while he whipped the audience into a frenzy, and I would watch on jealously from the bar. Not to worry, I thought, pretty soon I'll be up there on a par with you lot. One night, a presenter called Tony Emerson who, in all honesty, was hopeless and was permanently stuck on the graveyard shift, made an appearance and began shouting: "Who wants a free record?" Of course, the "Ow't for Now't" mob started screaming and putting their hands up to catch the discs he was flinging out. I was at the bar chatting to the club owner Gerald Summers when a punter pushed through the crowd and said, "You'd better get up there, he's giving your records away!" He showed me a record he had just grabbed and, sure enough, it had my name written on it. I turned to Gerald and he just shrugged his shoulders and said: "Johnny, it could be worse, he could be giving my records away."

CHAPTER ELEVEN: "Here Comes the Sun", Steve Harley and Cockney Rebel 1976 (Number 10)

I thought my six-week stint on BBC Radio Manchester went OK, I put a great deal of thought and effort into each show, but it just wasn't Radio Manchester. I didn't feature any councillors banging on about this, that or the other, there wasn't a cookery spot and no opportunities for the listener to flog his or her unwanted coffee table or sideboard. It was just me "muckin' about and playin' the music", much the same as I have ended up doing for the last 30-odd years of my working life. Basically, I was auditioning, unsuccessfully as it turned out, for a job on Piccadilly Radio. Having said that, I got no support whatsoever from anyone at the Beeb. I would go into the station every Friday night at 9.30pm, go on air at ten o'clock, finish at 11pm and leave at quarter past, and was never any the wiser as to what people thought about it. What I should have done is go into the radio station every day, knock on the boss's door, get my face known. What do they call it these days, networking? The thing is, back then I was just too shy, and I always felt that people earning their living in radio knew something I didn't. Of course, I now know that to be absolute rubbish. I got a rude awakening in the early 90s when I was working with a guy who had been a very prominent breakfast show presenter in Manchester for quite a few years. One day I was doing my show and I felt the need to turn the mic on and start singing along to the record. This bloke stormed into the studio and boomed, "Never do that on the radio, it's the first rule of broadcasting!" I was more than a bit embarrassed, until a few months later when I realised that this bloke's idea of show preparation was taking a giant joke book into the studio with him and, for instance, if he played 'Cathy's Clown' he'd find a joke about clowns and if he played 'Up The Ladder to the Roof' he'd find a joke about window cleaners. One day, he played Paul McCartney's minor hit 'Take It Away' so I'm thinking: "Go on mate, now what?" He somehow managed to find a gag about dustmen. After that I said to myself: "Stick your advice, pal, I'll do it my way." Anyway, back to Radio Manchester, I heard a few months later that half way through my stint, Derek Woodcock had been transferred to BBC Sheffield and his replacement immediately disowned the idea of "New Voices". So, it was back to the drawing board.

I was still very busy in the clubs, Thursday, Friday and Saturday was Pips whilst on Sundays and Wednesdays it was Tiffany's in Rochdale. Tiffany's was a very enjoyable place to work, always a decent crowd, especially on a Sunday. The only problem was that the young female assistant manageress enjoyed loudly entertaining one (or even two) punters in her locked office.

You ended up having to wait an hour or so before she'd unlock the door and casually, as if butter wouldn't melt, pay you your wages. One Monday morning I was still in Rochdale because I had spent the night at the flat of a very accommodating young lady who was apparently concerned that I shouldn't have to drive home. I pulled into a petrol station, put a couple of quid's worth of three-star in the old Beetle and, as I was walking back to the car, I became aware of two young girls risking life and limb by racing across the busy main road in my direction. "'Scuse Me, Mister," said one of the girls breathlessly "Are you David Essex?" Well, I gave her what I considered to be my best gypsy-style grin, got in the car and drove off. Those young girls will be in their 50s or 60s by now, mothers or maybe even grandmothers, but I bet to this day they are still not sure if, all those years ago, they really did bump into David Essex driving his ten-year-old VW Beetle in Rochdale on a Monday morning. Every week, record company reps would turn up at Pips with handfuls of free promotional records in the hope that we would give them a spin. 99% of these were rubbish, which I would save up until my car needed taxing and then sell for a few quid to a bloke on the market. The rep for EMI Records was a great bloke called Jeff Chegwin, who was the identical twin brother of the late TV Star Keith. One week, he turned up with two white label promo copies of The Sex Pistols infamous album 'Never Mind The Bollocks'. I played about 30 seconds of it, deemed it to be a load of old cobblers and gave one copy to the DJ in The Roxy/Weirdo room and sold the other one to the chap on the market, I think he gave me about 25p for it. Not sure how much a white label promo copy of that album would set you back these days, but you are certainly talking hundreds if not thousands of pounds. The man in charge of promoting CBS Records in the north west was a jovial bearded Welshman called Pen and on one visit he mentioned that he had heard the story of me playing David Essex's (him again) new record non-stop for an hour and, what with David being on the CBS label, Pen thought this was a brilliant wheeze and, as a consequence, had recommended me to Angels night club in Burnley, who were looking for a new 'Jock'. Now, I know what you're thinking - Burnley hardly sounds like the pulsating epicentre of the disco world and normally I would agree with you, but Angels had just been voted North West Nightclub of the Year and either second or third best in the entire country. They also paid very decent money, and the idea definitely appealed to me, so in November 1976 I started work as the new big shot at Angels. The local paper did a two-page spread, my ugly mush was on posters all over town, I was even introduced to the crowd before Burnley Football Club played Hull City at Turf Moor. I did feel a bit like Billy Big-Time, but that's how important Angels night club was to the people of Burnley.

Angels was a great place to work, always packed and never any trouble. The only fly in the ointment was that the previous DJ had been promoted to manager and he was convinced that he had written the book on how to do the job. I soon realised that he was a two-faced so-and-so who I would need to keep an eye on. I got on very well with the doormen, two of whom played football for local non-league side Padiham Town and fairly soon I was joining them in training on a Thursday evening before the club opened. Before I knew it, I was in the team. The standard of football was excellent, and the camaraderie was spot on, I loved it.

I rented a poky little flat opposite the police station and next door to a pie factory. If they were making chicken pies the smell was to die for, but on cheese and onion days, not so appetising. My mum bought me a portable black and white television set that I was genuinely delighted to get. Can you imagine young people today being grateful for a black and white portable telly? I would travel down to Burnley on the Thursday, stay until Sunday, then go back home with my dirty washing. One Friday night we had a Tramps Ball and, of course, I got into the spirit and turned up as Charlie Chaplin. As I mentioned earlier, back in the 70s drinking and driving wasn't frowned upon like it is now and I did end up having a couple of pints plus a couple of Harvey Wallbangers. Cocktails were all the rage at Angels and I soon found that a Harvey Wallbanger (Galliano, vodka and orange juice) was very much to my liking. Driving back to my flat at almost three in the morning dressed as Chaplin I suddenly became aware that a police car was behind me. My heart sank and I swallowed something hard and jagged. Aware that a number of police officers frequented Angels I staggered out of the car and said to the young copper: "I'm the disc jockey at Angels, we've had a Tramps Ball, I only live two minutes away." Sternly he told me to lock my car up and then he said: "It's your lucky night, I'll give you a lift home, but it'll cost you a VIP membership." "No Probs," I replied and jumped in the passenger seat. Like I said, different times.

I was called into a meeting one Tuesday afternoon to discuss plans for a testimonial dinner that was booked in for later in the month. The dinner was for the former Burnley centre forward Frank Casper, who had recently announced his retirement, and the guest speaker was to be comedian Frank Carson. It was a big occasion and the manager was determined that it should go without a hitch. The meeting dragged on for hours and didn't eventually finish until nearly eight o'clock at night. I decided to have something to eat at a New York-style burger bar that had recently opened in the town centre, it was a new concept in a small town and had really taken off as the place to be seen. I was feverishly tucking into my burger and fries when I noticed two very attractive girls walk in. I knew them both from the club, they were regulars. When I say I knew them, I don't mean in the biblical sense, just to say 'hello' to, that's all. One of the girls in particular was stunning and I had made a mental note sometime earlier that she was by a million miles the best-looking girl in Burnley. The restaurant was packed, and I was sitting on my own, so the girls came over and asked if they could join me. Now I hate eating with people I don't know and under normal circumstances this would have made me feel uncomfortable but the best-looking girl in Burnley and all that... "Please, sit yourselves down," I smiled. I can't for the life of me remember why the other girl left, but I found myself alone with the stunner and she seemed to like me. We chatted a lot and flirted quite a bit and I couldn't believe that she seemed so happy to be in my company. We made our way to the bar for a couple of cocktails, like I said earlier it seemed that the people of Burnley had just discovered the delights of Singapore Slings, Screwdrivers, Harvey Wallbangers and the rest. As the evening developed, we got quite giggly and touchy-feely and I really could not believe my luck. Here I was with Burnley's number one sex goddess and she amazingly seemed to be very happy in my company. Out of the blue she asked me if I'd like to go back to her place for a coffee. I didn't fancy a coffee, but I certainly fancied her. With my recent experience with the police officer at three in the morning still fresh in my mind, I decided to leave the car and get a taxi, the last thing I wanted was a pull from the Old Bill and have this chance of a lifetime cruelly snatched away. It turned out that she lived in a lovely big house on the edge of town, a house that perfectly matched the girl - beautiful.

It has to be said that she seemed in no mood for small talk and before I knew it, we were in the bedroom, clumsily if not erotically tearing each other's clothes off. We were both totally starkers when I heard a car enter the driveway. She jumped up and looked out of the window. "Shit," she exclaimed "It's my husband!" Husband? What husband? There had been no mention of a husband, but thinking about it later, why would a young single girl be living alone in such a big expensive place? She pulled on a dressing gown, said something like "We're both dead" and ran downstairs. What was I supposed to do? Perhaps I could try and make him understand that I didn't know he existed or perhaps I could do a naked shimmy down the drainpipe and leg it home, praying that nobody would see me. I have no idea why I made the decision, apart from blind panic, to hide under the bed, but that is what I did, leaving my clothes scattered all over the bedroom. I must have been under that bed for all of three minutes, but it genuinely felt like three hours. I was sure that the irate husband would storm into the bedroom any second, drag me from under the bed and beat the living daylights out of me. I can honestly say that I had never been in such a blind panic before, or indeed since. Eventually I heard the door close and the car drive off. Maybe he'd walked out on his wife, sick and tired of her wanton ways, maybe he was past caring which poor sucker was hiding under the bed this time, maybe he had just had enough. Or maybe he'd gone to borrow a gun and kill us both. The Burnley beauty, who by now had lost all her allure, raced back to the bedroom and gave me a filthy look as if to say, "Fancy scuttling under the bed, you wally". As I quickly got dressed, she explained that she had told her hubby she had gone to bed with a migraine, and would he please go and find an all-night chemist. He fell for it, proving that there is a God, and I got out of there as quickly as I could and began the long walk back to my car. When I got there, I had been given a parking ticket, a small price to pay under the circumstances. The girl continued to come into the club every weekend, but the best we could both manage was a nod and a knowing smile. On the night of Frank Casper's testimonial she turned up with her husband, who I recognised right away - he was a Manchester United defender who had fairly recently been signed from Burnley, and he was a big lad! I have told the story of the time I found myself hiding under a footballer's bed many times on the radio over the years and, of course, people are eager to know the name of the player. I would dearly love to name names but what if they are still together? It could have serious consequences, and even if they are not, Burnley's not that far away and, like I said, he's a big strong bloke and I don't fancy coming face to face with him down a dark alley, so his name must stay a closely guarded secret. Although, as Lloyd Grossman used to say, "All the clues are there".

While at Angels I got pally with a really nice guy called Steve Turner who was a DJ at a rival club and we shared a few boozy lunches, usually on a Friday. One Friday we were in the aforementioned burger bar and Steve ordered spare ribs. He called the waiter over, complaining that there was hardly any meat on his ribs. "Would you like to see the manager," said the harassed young waiter. "Only if he's got any meat on him," came the reply. Quite a witty retort, don't you think? But on top of three or four pints of lager, I thought it was the funniest thing I'd ever heard and was still chuckling two days later. Small things and all that. It was announced in the papers that Andy Peebles was to be the new soul music presenter on Radio One, which meant that he would be leaving Piccadilly Radio, where he did the same job. I put my application in the same day along with a demo tape. I mentioned that I was the DJ at one of the country's top discos and that I was an 'expert' on soul music. Within a couple of days, I got a phone call inviting me for an interview. I was interviewed once again by the dreaded Colin Walters. It was the second time he had interviewed me, and it didn't go any better this time around. It was a case of me getting tongue-tied at interview again and really letting myself down. Colin did say he wasn't going to give me the job, partly because they didn't have any black presenters on board, and he thought it was time they had one. I'm not sure you could get away with that nowadays, but I immediately thought about my old friend and colleague from Pips, Mike Shaft, and I couldn't wait to get around to his house and tell him about this great opportunity. I was delighted when Mike got the gig, not a hint of jealousy or resentment from me. Mike has gone on to have a great career in radio, he's a proper bloke and I love him to bits, and anyway, Mike would be able to return the favour some ten years later.

What I didn't realise was that a few weeks earlier Mike had been offered and accepted a job on an English-speaking radio station in Majorca. Of course, he now couldn't take up the offer to work abroad, but he kindly promised to put a good word in for me. When I told my mum that I was off to Spain to work on the radio, she wasn't exactly supportive. It was her usual reaction - why didn't I put this DJ malarkey to bed and get myself a proper job with a good pension - after all, I wasn't getting any younger. Over the years I wish I had a pound for every time she said to me, "Oh, our John, when are you going to get yourself a proper job?" If I had, I probably wouldn't need a pension. Having said that, she may well have been quite relieved that I was taking myself off to sunny Spain because for the last few months she had been "walking out" with a new man and they seemed very much in love. This new chap was also called John, but he could not have been more different from my dad. John number two was a real gentleman with a very good management job at Shell, nothing was too much trouble for John where my mum was concerned. They would end up travelling the world, enjoying fabulous holidays, quite a change from the Squires Gate Caravan Park. I think John was keen to move in with Mum and, goodness knows, she deserved some good fortune. It would be easier for both of them if I were out of the picture. The rest of Mum's family didn't really take to John, they thought he was a bit stuck up and compared to my dad he certainly was. Auntie Angie especially took an instant dislike to him, and mum and Angie had a big falling out and sadly never spoke to each other again. John was certainly a bit of a shock to the system after putting up with dad for all those years, but I came to really like him and more importantly he worshipped Mum and treated her like gold. When he died on the same day that Stanley Matthews passed away, it was such a shock, because he was so full of energy and they both had everything going for them. Mum went downhill fast after John's death and was never really the same person.

Interviews for the Majorca job had taken place at the Midland Hotel in the centre of Manchester, something I knew nothing about. The radio station was planning on going on air twenty-four hours a day rather than twelve and they needed three new people. As well as Mike, they hired a lad called Ed Simons another club DJ who I knew to say 'hello' to, but we certainly weren't friends, although that would change when we got to Spain. Ed was a fantastic bloke with a great temperament and, as I was about to find out, a total 'babe magnet'. There was a third bloke booked on the plane, but as it turned out he never showed up, so instead of three there were just the two of us. Me and my new friend Eddie arrived at Palma Airport mid-afternoon and we were both excited and a little nervous, taking our first tentative steps into what we both hoped would be a career in radio.

As we descended the steps of our Dan Air plane to be snapped by a dozen or so photographers, we had to remind ourselves that we were not having our photos taken because we were about to become household names, but because this was 1978 and every holidaymaker gets his or her photo taken leaving the plane, whether they like it or not, on the off chance they will purchase it just before the return journey. Eddie and I were both thinking the same thing, but both hoping that it would be quite a while before we would have to consider going home.

We were met by two tall well-dressed tanned middle-aged men, one a Canadian bloke called Bob, the other obviously a Spaniard called Paco. They both greeted Eddie like some kind of long-lost brother, while seeming to eye me up suspiciously. I started to feel like some kind of interloper: "Maybe they think I'm just some idiot loner who has just latched on to a new friend in Eddie?"

"Hello, I'm Johnny," I shouted enthusiastically. "Who?" said Bob and Paco, as one voice. It turned out that they had no idea who I was or what I was doing presenting myself in their country as some kind of would-be radio presenter.

It soon dawned on me that Mike had either forgotten to make the phone call or decided to let me sink or swim in Spain, so instead of welcoming a tall, black, cool dude with the proper DJ name of Mike Shaft onto their radio station, they were lumbered with a short arse called Johnny Owen who was stone white.

Amazingly, after a few minutes they did seem to be cool with it, and Bob drove us to the radio station for a quick look round before heading to the apartment that had been provided for us as part of the deal. 'Apartmentos Roses' was a two-bedroom flat on the third floor facing snow-covered mountains in Palma Nova. The deal was that we would be paid £100 a week with the apartment thrown in. What we didn't realise at the time was that we would be working for the Majorcan Mafia, essentially a father and his three sons who owned just about every bar, shop and restaurant in Palma Nova and Magaluf, which meant that we never paid for a single drink or meal in all the time we were working there, so the hundred pounds a week was hardly ever touched.

Eddie suggested we find a phone box so he could telephone his mum to let her know he had arrived safely and was fine. I'm so glad that he made the suggestion because I was so full of it that I would never have thought to call my mum, but when I did she was so relieved. She had been "on pins" - Mum was always "on pins", bless her.

Like I said, I knew Eddie to say 'hello' to in Manchester, because he was well-known on the local club scene, but now we had been thrown together he seemed like a really good guy and I was happy that we would get on fine. We were to start work on Monday, so the weekend was a finder-outer. We went for a meal and a few drinks then onto one of the clubs owned by 'the family'. We stumbled back to the apartment at well past three in the morning, full of spaghetti bolognese, Spanish plonk, cheap local whisky and we hadn't put our hands in our pocket once - happy days!

Now, I don't know if it was the euphoria or the booze that made me come up with this idea, but I've regretted it to this day: a league table of notches on the bedpost. We sellotaped a piece of A4 paper to the wall, drew a line down the middle and wrote Johnny at the top of one half and Eddie at the top of the other half. As The Beatles once said, "I should have known better". Eddie's mum was Maltese, so he had an olive complexion that made him look like he had lived in the Mediterranean all his life, he was tall, great-looking and, as I was about to find out, most of the young girls on the island shared my opinion. Added to this was the fact that 'The Family' quickly decided that Ed would be a far bigger asset dee-jaying in their number one money spinner The Borsalino disco in the very heart of Magaluf, where his good looks and easy charm could be fully appreciated by the female punters. As a result, Ed was very quickly on page two of our A4 "notches" board before I'd even sharpened my pencil. The radio station had changed its name from Radio Nova to Radio 24 in anticipation of going on the air around the clock. The station was the brainchild of Canadian Bob who had previously run an English-speaking newspaper aimed at the ex-pats. He had closed the paper down and opened the radio station some two years earlier, but it was the family who controlled the purse strings. They had provided the money, mainly to advertise their many businesses and it soon became clear that Bob constantly had to justify its existence.

Because the intended three extra presenters was now down to one, it meant that I usually had to do two shows a day. Normally one till four in the afternoon then the dreaded graveyard marathon: midnight till seven in the morning, seven days a week. It was certainly a crash course in radio presenting, but something I felt would stand me in very good stead in the future. Bob was loud and gregarious and loved his brandy, and quite often he would stumble into the studio at three in the morning after a night in the clubs, insisting that I play Meatloaf's 'Bat out of Hell' album and turn the mic on while he sang along at the top of his voice. We never got any complaints, which made me worry that nobody was actually listening.

On another occasion, Bob wandered into the studio with a bottle of Jack Daniels and said, "Son, I like you, you are doing a great job. Holy shit, some of the things you come out with crack me up!" I sensed a 'but' was coming, and I was right. "But the thing is," he continued, "You'll never get anywhere in this business with a name like Johnny Owen, that's a crap name for a jock." I didn't say anything but quietly I was agreeing with him, indeed in the weeks leading up to my debut on Radio Manchester I had toyed with the idea of changing it to something a bit more show biz. First I came up with 'Little Stevie Earle' which, to this day, I think is still a great name. Then I considered Scott Carpenter, which I believe I ripped off from one of the early astronauts. Then I decided I needed a name that was short and to the point, a name that didn't sound made up, and one that would sound great on a jingle. Piccadilly Radio had presenters such as Phil Wood, Pete Baker and Dave Ward which, while they were very ordinary names, they sounded great on the sung station jingles, so with that in mind I settled on John Ryder. I could hear them singing it in my mind. One afternoon while round at my Nana and Grandad's house I announced my new radio name. Nana wasn't best pleased. "But if we hear you on the wireless, we won't know it's you," she said, with considerable logic. Then, without putting down his Daily Mirror, my Grandad piped up, which was something he only did once in a blue moon. While Nana could talk the legs off a centipede, her husband would choose his words carefully, either that or he could never get a word in. "Johnny Owen's a good, strong, working-class name, don't be ashamed of it, lad." So, there it was, Johnny Owen it was and Johnny Owen it would stay, although Bob had other ideas. "From next week we are going to bill you as 'Captain Midnight', what do you think about that?" I muttered something about being stuck with a name like 'Captain Midnight' would mean that I would be consigned to presenting the graveyard shifts on radio forever more. After considering what I'd said for a while, Bob reluctantly agreed that I might have a point, and he said that we should get together the next day and come up with a name that we could both live with, before staggering off into the night with the parting shot: "Johnny Owen has got to go". Thankfully, once the Jack Daniels had worn off, he seemed to forget all about it and never mentioned it again, and neither did I.

Our apartment was situated above a restaurant which, surprise, surprise, was also owned by the family, so we ate there most days, free of charge, of course. We were aware that we were not expected to take liberties, so it was usually an omelette for lunch and garlic chicken for dinner. We got quite pally with a couple of young girls from London who, despite being permanently skint, were determined to do anything to stay in Majorca rather than go home. They cleaned private apartments and cleaned in bars and clubs but always seemed to be getting the sack. Ed and I came to the conclusion that they were probably a couple of petty thieves who couldn't resist helping themselves to any loose change they found lying around, but we felt a bit sorry for them and would give them a few pesetas for a meal whenever we could. One of the girls eventually gave up the struggle and decided to go back to London but the other stayed on. Then one day, out of the blue, she disappeared, and we had no idea what might have happened to her. We had visions of her being found murdered on the beach, but after about a month she turned up in a right old state, her face covered in serious burns. It turns out that she had blagged her way into a job as an exotic fire eater at a night club in the Majorcan capital of Palma, and just a few seconds into her debut, she went up in flames!

Meanwhile, I had started seeing a lovely Norwegian girl who was working as an au-pair. Pretty soon things became fairly serious and we were inseparable. There was even talk of an engagement. She was truly a fair-haired Nordic beauty and between you, me and the bed post, I couldn't keep my hands off her. I just wish I could remember her name! One night I noticed two lads drinking at the bar and I recognised one of them straightaway, it was Dave Bartram, the lead singer of chart-topping rock 'n' rollers Showaddywaddy. I went over and introduced myself and asked him if he'd consider coming on my afternoon show on the radio. He was very affable and agreed right away. He came on the very next day, I played a couple of his records, we had a good old natter and went for a drink after the show. What a top bloke, I thought. A few nights later I was in the Borsalino with my Norwegian girlie along with Dave and his mate, who were in there as well. We had a few drinks, had a bit of a laugh, took some pictures, which sadly I have since lost, then I noticed that time was getting on and I needed to get to the studio for my graveyard shift. As I kissed my lovely girlfriend good night, Dave slapped me on the back and said: "Don't worry, mate, I'll look after her." Hmm.

The following day we were having lunch in our freebie restaurant when out of the corner of my eye I noticed my beloved walking towards the beach. Something wasn't quite right. She was arm-in-arm with another bloke, and I recognised him immediately, it was my new show biz friend from Showaddywaddy. Miss Norway didn't see me, mainly because her eyes were closed, and she seemed to have got her tongue stuck down his throat. In fairness, he had promised me that he would look after her, and he seemed to have taken on the task with enthusiastic gusto. Showaddywaddy had indeed stolen my girl.

CHAPTER 12: "Leaving on a Jet Plane", Peter Paul and Mary 1970 (Number 2)

Just before we left for Majorca, Ed had started seeing a girl called Holly, indeed he talked about little else while we were there, apart from when he was busy entertaining other excitable female holidaymakers that is. Holly was an aspiring singer who had just signed a recording deal. While we were out there she appeared on Top of the Pops singing her debut single which, in truth, was a run-of-the-mill piece of disco fodder, which got lost in the midst of the thousands of other disco-aimed records that were being released in the wake of Saturday Night Fever.

After a few weeks of endless letters and phone calls being exchanged between the pair of them, Holly agreed to come over and spend a week at our apartment. I have to agree with Ed, she was a stunner, a statuesque, long-legged beauty with a winning smile and a good personality. It wasn't too difficult to understand why he had become so besotted. To be honest, I didn't see a lot of Ed and Holly while she was staying with us, maybe they contracted a virus or something but they seemed to spend most of their time in bed. After we waved her off at Palma Airport, Ed was even more lovesick than before, absence would indeed make the heart grow fonder. One night, I was on the air, half way through my graveyard shift and, as usual, Canadian Bob was in the studio, a little bit worse for wear. He seemed uncharacteristically down, and he told me he was getting grief from the family about the lack of advertising on the station and he wasn't sure how much longer they would be prepared to back him. I had already started to worry that our weekly wages were becoming more and more difficult to get our hands on. When we first started, everything was great, we would report to a souvenir shop in Palma Nova on a Friday afternoon and Paco the patriarch, who had an office in the back, would appear with our wage packets, paid in full, no questions asked. Just lately, however, we would end up waiting all day only to be told that we wouldn't get paid until the Monday, then the Monday would become the Tuesday, then the Wednesday, and so on. The money was always forthcoming but it was becoming worryingly slipshod. I put Elvis Costello's minor hit 'Radio Radio' on the turntable and this seemed to temporarily cheer up Bob and he told me a story that I repeated once on Signal Radio many years later and it very nearly got me the sack. According to Bob this incident had happened live on air a few days earlier during the breakfast show on a leading London-based radio station. The presenter was running a competition in which the listener could win quite a lot of money. The idea was that the listener could ask a number of questions that would help them identify the 'famous mystery person'. Don't forget, this was live on the air at breakfast time. The listener had already established that the mystery person in question was a well-known sports presenter. The answer, incidentally, was Murray Walker, but the female listener was a bit stumped, so the presenter decided to give a couple of clues. First, he started humming the tune to the famous Murray Mints advert; you know the one, "Murray Mints, Murray Mints, too good to hurry mints." This failed to ring any bells with the listener so, desperately running out of time, the presenter tried to help once again. "His first name is the same as something you put in your mouth and suck," he said. "You've got ten seconds," he added. "I've got it!" said the excited listener, already planning how to spend the cash. "I know who it is! It's … Dickie Davies!"

Out of the blue, one wet, overcast and depressing afternoon, Ed announced that he could no longer survive without Holly and he was going home. I had never thought about leaving because here I was, finally living the dream. I was a fully-fledged professional radio presenter, but I found myself saying, "Well, if you're going, I might as well come with you." I regretted it as soon as the words had left my lips, but it was too late, and before I knew it we were on the plane home. I mentioned earlier that because all our meals and drinks were free we hardly needed to spend any money and because we weren't sure about the Spanish rules and regulations regarding taking money out of the country we ended up hiding thousands of pesetas in our shoes and socks, tucked in the bottom of our luggage.

The second we landed in Manchester, I felt sick. It was cold, it was chucking it down, I was no longer a radio presenter, in fact, I was nothing. No job at all. My only comfort was that I had a few quid stuffed down my socks. Insult was added to injury a few days later when a downcast Ed told me that Holly had moved in with another disc jockey and Ed was yesterday's news.

So here I was, back living at home with Mum and her new love, John. As charming as he was, I soon got the impression that John was uncomfortable with this arrangement and I definitely knew where he was coming from. I promised them both that I would move out as soon as possible. One morning, while Mum and John were both at work, there was a knock on the door. It was a stern looking middle-aged lady from the Inland Revenue with a tax demand for me. Thanks very much, I thought, that's all I need. It meant that the money I had saved in Spain was virtually wiped out in one fell swoop. You could now add 'penniless' to 'jobless' to describe my circumstances.

I was enjoying a few glasses of Leibfraumilch in my favourite Manchester wine bar when somebody tapped me on the shoulder, it was my old Pips boss, Gerald Summers. We had a brief chat about Spain and this and that and, as he was leaving, he whispered, "Ring me in the morning".

It transpired that Gerald had recently taken over a new club. It had been a spacious old-fashioned cabaret bar called Romanoff's which unsurprisingly had gone bust. Because the letter "R" was engraved all over the carpets and, in order to save a few quid, Gerald needed a name for his new venture that began with that letter, and he had decided on Rotters. During our brief telephone conversation, he offered me the job of disc jockey, which I was in no position to turn down. After sampling life on the radio, I was less than enthusiastic about going back to club work but the radio world was hardly inundating me with offers.

A mate of mine called Ken was the manager of a Victoria Wine shop on the outskirts of Manchester and his job came with a flat just above the shop. Ken and his wife had decided to buy a house, which meant that they no longer needed the flat so they decided to rent it to me. It was a highly dubious practice and most certainly frowned upon by the directors of the Victoria Wine operation, but what they didn't know wouldn't hurt them, and I wasn't about to tell them. I happily agreed to pay Ken a tenner a week and I was able to move in straight away. I got right down to decorating the place. I painted the living room walls green to match the brown skirting board. A mate said it looked like the inside of one of those chocolate eclair sweets, but I thought it looked the business. I bought a couple of those popular Athena posters, the female tennis player scratching her bum adorned the wall above the fireplace and the chimpanzee sitting on the toilet reading the newspaper took pride of place in the bathroom. I loved that little flat and was very happy there, although I had to tread carefully whenever the area manager called into the shop below.

On my very first night at Rotters I got talking to a couple of girls, one of whom was especially friendly, and I asked her back to the flat for a 'coffee'. The entrance to the flat was up a fire escape round the back of the building, it was very dark and had quite a menacing feel about it, particularly in the middle of the night. The girl would later admit that she was genuinely in fear of her life. This bloke she had never seen before had taken her to this bleak, unforgiving place and he surely had murder in mind. I have often joked that the reason I ended up marrying my first wife was because she came back to my flat and refused to go home. To be honest, I was only half joking. Her mother had shacked up with a layabout half her age who would regularly try it on with Elaine. So, yes, the young girl I took back to my flat that night would never go home and would become the mother of my child and then my wife. Elaine's mother and father had split up some years earlier and although I took an immediate dislike to her mother, I quite liked her dad. He was a cheerful chappie who wore a toupee, but only at weekends. Meanwhile, I was going through the motions at Rotters, but I'd truthfully had quite enough of discos and longed to get back on the radio so after a few months Gerald Summers and I decided to part company. I devoted all my time to trying to get a job on Piccadilly Radio who, by this time, had a new programme controller called Tony Ingham. I inundated poor Tony with demo tapes and was in his office almost every week hoping for a job. Tony was of the opinion that although my tapes were good he thought I was just too nervous to go on air. Seemingly nothing could persuade him otherwise. A lot of this was my fault, I was still hopelessly tongue-tied at interviews, scared to say the wrong thing. At the start of every interview, Tony would offer me a cup of tea and the cup would be visibly shaking in my hand, which certainly didn't help matters. Eventually I stopped saying 'yes' to the tea. Working on Piccadilly Radio, my local station, meant so much to me, I completely went to pieces the moment I entered the building. On one occasion Tony suddenly said that he need somebody for overnights next week and would I be up for it? I must have hesitated for a split second because right away he followed it up with, "No, you're a bag of nerves I can't trust you." It was that salted snail feeling all over again. However, Tony did offer me a job, of sorts, as a part-time technical operator. I had no idea what that entailed but I was more than happy to give it a go. I soon discovered that a better name for technical operator would have been low-paid dogsbody. The job mainly consisted of making the tea, manning the telephones and generally waiting on the on-air staff hand and foot, all for two quid a shift. Not an hour, a shift. So, I found myself running around after the late night presenter and then the overnight presenter, 10pm till 6am, two or three nights a week. The overnight presenters on Piccadilly Radio at the time seemed to be a collection of chancers who could talk the talk, probably very plausible in interviews, but pretty clueless on-air. One night, I was working with a chap called Mike Day, another holder of the short, sharp sounds-great-on-jingles-type name, who was typical of the breed. Mike had been a club disc jockey, a pub landlord and was now working as a part-time taxi driver. One of my key jobs, especially in the middle of the night, was to vet the callers to make sure they weren't pie-eyed before letting them loose on the radio. One night a woman phoned up and although she was a bit giggly I put this down to nerves and, despite my concerns, decided to put her through to Mike. It soon became obvious that the woman was indeed the worse for wear and the presenter was already throwing me daggers when, out of nowhere, she suddenly blurted out "fucking hell, my chip pans on fire" before slamming the phone down.

This was the beginning of the 1980s, my least-favourite decade. Everything I seemed to try in the 80s ended in tears, including my marriage. The only real great thing to happen was the birth of my son Marc on the 19th of June 1981. I'll be honest with you and say that when Elaine announced that she was pregnant, I was less than delighted, I wasn't exactly happy, money was tight and it was the last thing I needed, but the moment I laid eyes on him in his little incubator in Stepping Hill Hospital in Stockport my heart just melted. This was my son, my own flesh and blood and he was gorgeous. Marc was born seven weeks premature weighing in at less than a bag of sugar, in fact the nurses nicknamed him Tate and Lyle. I missed the birth because I had agreed to cover for a mate of mine who was going on a stag night. My mum's new partner John had been all over Manchester trying to find me, running in and out of every nightclub in town. When I did get to the hospital, the first thing the doctor said was, "He's very weak, he's got a hole in his heart and it's touch and go." I put my hand in the little hole in the incubator and Marc grabbed hold of my finger, I realise now that this is just a natural reaction but to me it was my newborn son saying 'hello' to his daddy and I just burst into tears.

I think my hatred of the 1980s contributed to my decision to leave the Signal Radio Breakfast Show many years later. Even though the station was doing very well, the powers-that-be made the decision to ditch most of the 60s and 70s hits and replace them with 80s songs instead. The song rotation was so small that I seemed to be playing the same songs every morning. Many people still think that radio presenters choose their own music, but this is quite the opposite of what goes on these days. When I first started on the radio you would go in the record library, choose a selection of songs and, added to the records already play-listed, that was your show for the day. But for years now it's all been about focus groups and research, the presenter has no say, in fact he or she is never even consulted, which I have always found to be ridiculous. Including both clubs and radio, I have been playing music professionally for 45 years and I have never been asked what I thought about a particular song. I think this stems from the fact that so-called "hot" FM stations employ presenters who, because they are so young and have never really experienced that much of the outside world, they simply cannot be trusted to choose their own music. Another thing that I've noticed over the years is that every single Programme Controller I have ever worked for was previously a very ordinary presenter who really couldn't wait to get into management, whereas great presenters are usually committed to just making great radio programmes. At Signal we were told that if you had something interesting to talk about save it until ten minutes to the hour! How ridiculous is that? I like to think that most of my links were either interesting or funny or preferably both. For the uninitiated, a link is the presenter's bit in-between the music. In 1992, I was invited to go to Florida and host a week of shows from Walt Disney World, and I noticed that most of the presenters on American radio stations were in their 50s and 60s but were treated with the utmost respect. Here in England, once you get to 40 you are looking over your shoulder. The best you can hope for is to be moved to a station on the medium wave. The bosses at Signal dubbed their medium wave offering, Signal Two, 'God's waiting room', which I always hated and could never understand. Older listeners are the ones with the money, they have most likely paid off their mortgage, their kids have flown the nest and at last, having worked hard all their lives, they have a bit of disposable income. They are the age group that advertisers should be targeting, but all the promotion and money was spent on the FM station, Signal One, with their target audience of under-30s. For most of my career, I have been lucky enough to work for programme controllers who understood and trusted me and gave me quite a lot of leeway where the music was concerned. Much as I always wanted to work on radio, I simply couldn't go into the studio every day and play the same handful of songs usually in the same order that I had played the day before. When these focus groups put a tick against a certain song, they simply don't realise that they are signing up to hear the same song every day for the next few years. By and large, I never had a problem with my programme controllers because I always delivered healthy audiences. No, it was *their* bosses that I've always had trouble with. Don't get me started! Now, where was I??

With Marc's arrival, we decided to get married and buy a house. Despite having no money and no prospects, it seemed the right thing to do. We eventually settled on a little terraced house in Ashton-under-Lyne, a small market town on the edge of east Manchester. The price was £10,500. Cheap and cheerful, but it felt like a fortune at the time. We moved in on the 12th of June 1981, as it turned out just a week before Marc's premature arrival. The following weekend was quite memorable, Marc was born on the Friday, on the Saturday I won a grand on the football pools and on the Sunday I celebrated my first ever Father's Day. I consider myself something of an expert when it comes to football but the only time I ever won the pools was in the close season when the only results you could bet on were the Australian ones. It was a case of putting your cross down and keeping your fingers crossed. That one thousand pounds certainly came at a good time, we were able to buy a cheap three-piece suite and a few other bits and pieces for our new home.

Early in 1984 I got a phone call from a chap called Charles Turner, he was setting up a radio station which would be based in Stockport. The only problem was that he had no licence so the station would, in effect, be a pirate radio station, just like the old days of Radio Caroline and all that. Charles assured me that there was a loophole in the rules, which meant he could easily get round the license situation. Charles was very impressive and I promised to get back to him the next day. I had been recommended by a friend of mine from the club scene called Pete Smith, so I went round to Pete's house for a chat. Pete was pencilled in to do the mid-morning show but they still needed someone to do Breakfast and he had very kindly put my name forward. I was a bit worried about the pirate aspect but the more I thought about it the more it appealed. At least Tony Ingham might hear me and realise that I was perfectly able to hold down a radio show. I telephoned Charles and agreed to present the all-new KFM Radio Breakfast Show.

Charles Turner had recruited some very talented people for this exciting new station. They included Craig Cash, who would go on to write and star in The Royle Family and Early Doors; Jon Ronson, who would become a best-selling writer and TV presenter; Norman Beaker, a well-respected blues singer and songwriter, who would host the weekly rhythm and blues show; Ray King, who would go on to present 'Pub of the Week' with Mel Scholes on Signal Radio; and Rob Charles, who would have a great career in radio in the ensuing years. KFM would only last about twelve months before the authorities closed the loophole and ultimately shut the station down, but in that time we became the station to listen to, and made damaging inroads into Piccadilly Radio's listening figures, so much so that anybody working on KFM would be blacklisted by Piccadilly for many years. So much for my Tony Ingham theory, but I loved working on KFM, it was genuinely ground-breaking and very exciting. There were many highlights but probably the biggest one was interviewing the great George Best. He was doing a book signing in Woolworths and the interview was set up to take place in the stores stockroom. George's manager suggested I take a bottle of wine, just to break the ice. To be on the safe side, I took two bottles - I had a glass and George took care of the rest. To be honest, George wasn't on great form at this time, it was shortly before he was arrested and sent to prison for assaulting a police officer, but on the day he was good-humoured and very good value. He even presented me with a signed copy of his book, which I have to say seemed to have been pieced together with the sole intention of making a quick buck. It was, sadly, a lousy read.

I did manage to get a week off from presenting the breakfast show to take Elaine and Marc on holiday to Magaluf. One day I went off to find my old radio station, but when I got there it was no more. It had been turned into a bar and bistro, no doubt owned by the family, although I did manage to bump into Canadian Bob on the last day, and he told me he was doing fine working as a singer in one of the local bars, God help the punters! The holiday was unremarkable apart from the time my two-and-a-bit year old son really needed a poo and unfortunately the fact that he was in the hotel swimming pool at the time could not be allowed to get in the way.

1984 ended with what could have been a tragedy, if not for my son saving the day. The weather was terrible at Christmas that year, Britain was knee-deep in snow and it was bitterly cold. I put an electric blanket on Marc's bed to warm it up and turned it off before putting him down - or at least I thought I did. In the middle of the night, Marc came into our bedroom to say his room was full of smoke. In my sleepy haze, I tried to shoo him away, but he was most insistent. Thank God he was, because by now his room was on fire, like a scene from The Towering Inferno. I got everybody downstairs and rang 999. Then I realised that I was stark naked so I stupidly attempted to go back upstairs, but by now that was impossible. We found ourselves sitting in our new neighbours' front room with cups of tea while the firefighters battled the blaze. Embarrassingly, all I had to cover my modesty was a hastily grabbed tea towel. We had to stay at my mum's house for a few weeks while the damage was repaired. Thankfully, we were insured and once the house had been done up it looked a lot nicer than it did before the fire.

Before too long our new neighbours, who had been so helpful that night, would turn into the neighbours from hell. First, he knocked a big hole in our kitchen wall while attempting a bit of DIY. He turned out to be the only man in the world who was a bigger do-it-yourself disaster zone than me. He promised to fix it right away, but it dragged on for weeks. I had to knock on his door and complain time and time again, until he eventually, and grudgingly, got it sorted. Then he got himself not one but two German Shepherd dogs and kept them locked up in his tiny back yard for most of the day and all of the night. Once again, I got sick of knocking on his door. One night we had just put Marc to bed when he threw the dogs in the yard and they immediately started again, I was straight round. In a bid to get him to see reason I told him that I had worked in nightclubs all my life and I knew some very dangerous people, any more trouble and he would know about it. He shrugged off my threats and said that where he came from they didn't talk about what they were going to do, they just shot people. My next-door neighbour was actually threatening to shoot me. I told Elaine and the first thing she said was, "I wonder where he comes from?" I never did find out and, thankfully, he never did carry out his threat.

Once KFM had been taken off the air, my prospects were once again looking bleak, and one of the reasons I have such bad memories regarding the 80s is that everything I tried just didn't work out. I could never really get going. It was a depressing time all round what with the street riots, the Falklands War, the miners' strike and the IRA. When Marc was born, I wanted to call him Sean, but my mum was dead against it, she thought it was too Irish and that people would have pre-conceptions because of the Irish troubles. Instead, I decided to name him after one of my musical heroes. Thirty-odd years later, Marc's beautiful Dublin-born wife, Jacqueline, would give birth to my gorgeous little grandson and call him Sean, so it all worked out well in the end. In 1985 I had the screwball idea of blowing my meagre life savings on opening a recording studio for disc jockeys, a place where we could make jingles and a place where aspiring radio presenters could make demo tapes. In hindsight, it was a half-baked idea, but I thought it might just supply me with a bit of a living. I invited my old KFM mate Pete Smith to come in with me. Pete had no money but he was pretty good technically and I didn't really feel confident enough to go it alone. Pete's a really nice guy but I think he suffered from what they call OCD (Obsessive Compulsive Disorder) and everything had to be just so. In the morning, I would go into the studio and move the telephone a couple of inches from where it usually sat just to see how long it would take Pete to move it back. It normally took about five seconds. The studio did OK for the first few months, but it soon became obvious that it wouldn't provide a living, certainly not for two of us. We reluctantly decided to sell up and, amazingly, the first person who came to see it agreed to buy the business. At least, he wanted to buy all the equipment and move the operation to his home town of Wolverhampton, which was fine by us. When he came to see us I got a mate to phone up every few minutes and I would have a conversation with this pretend 'customer' telling him that his order had been completed and it would be sent out that very day. We made it sound as if we were run off our feet and the potential buyer was taken in, hook, line and sinker. He came round for the second time on a Sunday morning, took all the gear away, and paid us in cash. Pete and I sat on the floor counting out the money like a couple of bank robbers: a tenner for you, a tenner for me, a tenner for you, a tenner for me. When we finished the count-up there was a ten pound note left so I said, "I'll have that" and put it in my pocket. Bloody hell, Pete went on about that for months, how I'd had the cheek to pocket the last tenner, completely ignoring the fact that I had ploughed my life savings into this business. He got 50% of everything we earned and never bought so much as a paper clip.

Amazingly, out of the blue I got a phone call from Tony Ingham who, by this time, had left Piccadilly under a bit of a cloud but had got the same job at Radio City in Liverpool. He wanted me to have a bash at the weekend breakfast show. I couldn't believe what I was hearing but it turned out he had been listening to me on KFM, after all, and loved what he heard. The only thing he was concerned about was how my Manchester accent would go down in Liverpool, so I argued that I really didn't have much of an accent, but he replied: "Don't be daft, you're a total Manc - but let's see how it goes."

All this was happening against the backdrop of my disintegrating marriage. I didn't want to be there and made no secret of it. We were arguing all the time and it must have been a horrible situation for Marc. Eventually, I moved into the spare bedroom, something would have to give. Sadly, Tony Ingham didn't last too long at Radio City and the incoming replacement decided a clear-out was needed, and I was one of the names on his list. I was told the news by telephone after one of my Saturday shows, the first and last time I would ever speak to the new guy. I was feeling very disappointed as I made my way back home, but as soon as I got through the door there was another unwelcome bit of news waiting for me. Elaine had hired a solicitor and there was a letter from him telling me that she was filing for divorce because of my unreasonable behaviour and I would have to vacate the marital home by the end of the month. This was a bombshell I just wasn't prepared for. By this time, I had a girlfriend, but my wife made no secret of the fact that she had a boyfriend. I gathered that she thought that if I was out of the way he would be only too happy to move in. As it transpired, when faced with the prospect of moving in and taking on somebody else's child, he was out of there like a shot, never to be seen again. I was prepared to continue as we had been doing, if only for Marc's sake, but her mind was made up. So, no business, no job and now no home. What the hell was I going to do now? It was looking as though I would have to get a proper job. At least my mum would be pleased about that.

I decided I had wasted enough time farting about as a disc jockey and, as my careers officer had warned all those years ago, it was time to join the real world. The main drawback was that, apart from 18 months as a shop assistant all those years ago, I had never had a proper job. Who would want to take me on?

I left home with just the spare telly and my record collection and rented a flat, but I was determined to buy a house, despite having no job and no prospects. I ended up putting a deposit down on the cheapest and most run-down old house I could find and the Nationwide Building Society gave me a mortgage. It's amazing what you can achieve with a bit of bravado and bullshit.

While I was busy contemplating what to do with the rest of my life, I read in the Manchester Evening News that my old mate Mike Shaft had been granted a license to open a soul music radio station, so I nipped round to say 'hello' and offer my congratulations. He said he had been trying to get hold of my phone number because he wanted me to do the afternoon drive time show. Mike was gobsmacked when I said I wasn't really interested, I told him I'd had quite enough of the uncertain world of radio and now wanted a quiet life in civvy street. We shook hands, wished each other well and I left. I was totally out of love with radio, but even I could hardly believe what I had just said. It took three telephone calls from Mike to finally convince me that radio was where I belonged and, with no other offers lined up, I genuinely reluctantly agreed to become the drive time presenter on the all-new Sunset Radio, broadcasting from the centre of Manchester. Apparently, Sunset Avenue was where Marvin Gaye was born. Despite the competition from the likes of Piccadilly Radio and others, Sunset was quite a success, and our first official listening figures showed that we had taken 15% of the available audience, and my show had 22%, so I was well pleased. I very much enjoyed my time at Sunset, the only problem was that what I called reverse racism was rife in the building. Most of the other presenters were loud, opinionated, young black guys who made it known at every meeting that they thought white people should not be allowed anywhere near a soul station.

As part of the new licences being issued, KFM was also back on the air in Stockport, this time part-owned by the same people who owned Signal Radio in Stoke, and one day I got a call from Signal's programme controller, John Evington. I had never previously spoken to John but I had received lots of rejection letters from him a few years earlier. It turned out that John had heard my show on the original pirate KFM and was keen to get me back on the station. You tend to bump into the same people time and time again in the radio business and it just so happened that I was being lined up to replace my old boss Ray Teret - the powers-that-be had finally lost patience with Ray thanks to his rather 'laissez-faire' attitude to presenting his show. Quite a few of the 1984 guys had also been brought back into the presentation line up, my OCD buddy Pete Smith, Craig Cash and Rob Charles, so I really felt at home right away. The boss was a chap called Neil Cossar, who for years had been the guitarist with the post-punk band The Cheaters. Neil's cheerful, laid-back approach helped to create a fantastic atmosphere in the building and it was a great place to work. I started doing the afternoon show on the 15th of October 1990 a date that was of great significance to me. My beloved Nana was born on that date, so was my Auntie Ethel, and it would be the date I started my record-breaking run on the Signal 2 breakfast show many years later. In 1992, a decision was taken to change the name of the station to Signal Cheshire following a conversation I had with John Evington. John was baffled by the fact that KFM was nowhere near as popular as it had been when it was a pirate station in the 80s. I said I thought the reason was obvious, people were drawn to the original station because it was technically illegal, in the same way that CB radio was incredibly popular until it was legalised, and then it died a death. I originally thought the name change was a mistake because the local paper kept referring to us as 'Stoke-based', which didn't go down too well with the locals. With the name change, Dave Johnson and Ray King were both added to the line-up. They were brought in from Signal in Stoke and, I'm ashamed to say, were both given a hard time by the rest of us. It was nothing personal, we just thought the changes were not needed. It was also the year Jon Keighren joined us as news editor. Jon is a little chap, the same size as me, who loves his football and enjoys a pint, much the same as me, and we quickly became firm friends, and I'm delighted and proud to say we are still best mates to this day. When Signal Cheshire began covering Stockport County's football matches, Jon and I formed a winning partnership, he was the commentator and I was the summariser. When I say summariser, that is to say I chipped in with some hopefully witty comments from time to time and generally got in the way of him doing his job. While driving to away games Jon would come up with a ludicrous phrase that I had to shoehorn into the commentary during the match. That is how, during a game against Queens Park Rangers I found myself saying, "The last time I saw such a dodgy tackle was in a Turkish bath house."

CHAPTER 13: "It's All Over Now", The Rolling Stones 1964 (Number One)

1992 was an interesting year. It's the year I played my Handshake Game on the radio for the first time. It was during an interview with the wonderful Kirsty McColl, who was completely baffled, but thankfully went along with it. Let me give you an example of how the handshake game works. It works best if you start off with a very minor celeb, for instance I once interviewed a local Stockport girl who, that weekend, had appeared on "Stars in Their Eyes" pretending to be Mary Hopkin. Of course, we shook hands before the show, as she would have shaken hands with the presenter of "Stars" Matthew Kelly. Matthew once appeared in a panto with Stephanie Powers who starred in *Hart to Hart* with Robert Wagner who was in a film with Katherine Hepburn who famously starred in *The African Queen* with Humphrey Bogart. Bogey was in a film with Ava Gardner who was married to Frank Sinatra who was very friendly with John F Kennedy, so for the purposes of the game I can go from that young girl in Stockport to shaking hands with the one and only JFK. That is how you play the Handshake Game. It's been a staple of my shows ever since that day in '92.

It was also the year I broke my leg, the only time I ever broke a bone in my body. The only saving grace was that I did it playing football. We had got a team together at Signal Cheshire playing anybody who would give us a game. We were scheduled to play a team from B&Q one Sunday evening and it was the one and only time I didn't fancy playing a game of football, in fact, I nearly didn't bother turning up. Of course, I did show up, fearful of the stick I'd get if I didn't. Two minutes into the match and a crunching tackle came in from behind, nobody had mentioned the word "friendly" to the B&Q lads. The crack echoed around the ground, people talk about late tackles, but this one was at least a day late. It wasn't until the following day that I was reminded that I was booked in to do a week of shows in America in about three weeks. Walt Disney World in Florida had just installed their exciting new Space Mountain ride and they had invited radio stations from all over the world to take part in a week-long celebration. Both Signal Radio in Stoke and Signal Cheshire were among the stations invited. Before breaking my leg, I was very excited about going to America and the prospect of actually broadcasting from there was a dream come true, but now I didn't fancy it at all. The idea of going off to the states in plaster just didn't appeal. I offered Cashy the chance to take my place but John Evington wouldn't hear of it, apparently my name had been used on billboards. Disney were expecting Johnny Owen, so Johnny Owen had to show up, broken leg or no broken leg.

Three of us were actually chosen to make the trip, I would represent Signal Cheshire alongside a young chap called Shaun Tilley, who was familiar to all Signal Stoke listeners and my boss Neil Cossar would be in charge of producing the shows and, I dare say, making sure we behaved ourselves. I had never met Shaun before, but he had a reputation for being a bit "big time". As it turned out he was a great guy, one of the lads, and all three of us had a whale of a time. Every night after the shows we would retire to Neil's room, order take away pizzas and get happily bladdered. I was fascinated by the people who worked at Disney, they all seemed to be the same age with the same teeth, the same permanent smile and the same total dedication to the job. One night, we were invited to a dinner in honour of the Chief Executive Michael Eisner, and when he entered the room it was as if Jesus himself had walked in. You genuinely got the impression that if he had ordered everyone to jump into alligator-infested waters, there would have been a queue of smiley faces eager to be the first one in. The Signal Radio stand was just one of hundreds from radio stations all over the world, including many from America itself. As I mentioned earlier, what struck me most about the American presenters was that most of them were in their 50s and 60s, but they were all treated like genuine celebrities and held in high esteem, very different from England. To this day, I remain extremely proud of the shows we did at Disney World, I thought we did a fantastic job although soon after we got back Shaun was sacked by John Evington and to this day I have no idea why, I thought he was a really good presenter and a top bloke. On the very last day the weather changed for the worse, a hurricane was heading our way and virtually blowing us off our feet. I was pleased to say that Signal Cheshire was still just about broadcasting when all the others had given up. The presidential election campaign was under way and Bill Clinton was looking like he was heading for the White House, and a producer from a station based in Milwaukee overheard a bit of my show and, fascinated by my accent, invited me to take part in a debate about Clinton. For half an hour I bluffed and blustered about the opinion British people had about the prospective new president, the only thing I remember saying was that "he looks a bit like Kennedy". Clearly Robin Day had nothing to worry about.

Neil Cossar cornered me one day to say he had just had a phone call from a man who was a real fan of the show, and because this man was out of work he had volunteered to come in and help out by making the tea, answering the phones and generally mucking in. Now I have never been of the opinion that presenting a radio show was any kind of spectator sport and I've always felt uncomfortable with having people In the studio. Nevertheless, I reluctantly went along with it. The next day the man turned up, and I got one of the shocks of my life, he was a Goth, dressed in black from head to foot, with dyed black hair, matching lipstick and fingernails. Never in a million years would I have identified him as a fan of the Johnny Owen Show, especially as at the time one of my most popular features was "the Tony Christie moment" which basically meant playing Tony's 1971 minor hit "Is this the way to Amarillo". This was a few years before the Peter Kay inspired revival and I dare say years before Peter had ever heard of Tony Christie. This weird looking bloke told me his name was Bela Lugosi and he had changed his name by deed poll because he was a big fan of the late horror star. In order to start up some kind of conversation I mentioned Bela's last film "Plan 9 from Outer Space", universally acknowledged as the worst film ever made and one in which Lugosi had dropped dead half way through to be replaced by the producer's dentist. Strangely, this incarnation of Bela had never heard of that film. After a while, the weirdo started to freak me out so I made my excuses, left the studio and told Neil to think of a way of getting rid of him. I was totally gobsmacked when two days later he was on the front page of the Manchester Evening News. He had been arrested for strangling his girlfriend, cutting her body up and dumping her in the cellar. It was sickening to think that the poor girl was actually in the cellar while he was in my studio casually bringing me cups of tea. This macabre incident did however provide me with one of my most popular phone-ins: "Have you ever met a murderer"? Not a subject you would normally hear on a family radio show, sandwiched between Bananarama and Take That, but you would not believe just how many ordinary people have indeed met at least one murderer.

I can't mention Signal Cheshire without talking about "The Pineapple", which was our local pub right next door, because we spent as much time in there as we did at work. It became known as 'Studio Three'. The "Chunky", as the locals called it, was a traditional working-class pub with a dart board and a juke box. It was run by Bill and Eileen, and a group of us would be in every day for a pint and a bit of lunch, then normally at just gone 6pm, after my show had finished, we were back there again. One of the more memorable locals was old Joe, a chap in his late 70s who would turn up every night just as we got there carrying a bunch of flowers. He would sit at an adjoining table so he could earwig our conversation. One night the talk turned to women, as it quite often did, and Joe piped up with: "I've never had a woman and never wanted one." A couple of nights later he piped up again: "I've had women from all over the world, all shapes and sizes, and all colours." "Bloody hell, Joe," laughed Craig Cash. "Make your mind up." I remember saying that The Pineapple would make a great subject for a sitcom, not realising that Cashy was already turning the idea over in his mind. Years later the Pineapple would become the Grapes as Craig's mini masterpiece "Early Doors" hit our TV screens.

During my seven years at Signal Cheshire, I was lucky enough to interview some very famous people. Let me talk you through some of them. Adam Ant was a bloke I took to right away, he was very friendly, if seemingly a bit confused. He kept on saying that we had met before and no matter how many times I assured him that if I had bumped into Adam Ant previously I would no doubt remember, he just wouldn't be told. I pre-recorded the interview and me, Cashy, Jon and Neil talked Adam into joining us in the Pineapple. In fairness to him he took it all in his stride and didn't bat an eyelid while the open-mouthed punters looked on in awe as he tucked into pie, chips and beans washed down with a pint of Robbies lager. Whether the locals were shocked to see Adam Ant in their local back-street boozer or whether they couldn't believe someone was actually having baked beans with pie and chips, I'll never know. Suddenly Adam came to life: "I've got it!" he exclaimed. "You're Howard Jones, we shared a dressing room on Top of The Pops." If you remember, Howard was a tall blonde-haired bloke but, like I said, Adam just wouldn't be told.

When Burger King opened a new branch in the centre of town, I was booked in to do a live show from there on the opening day. The franchise owner turned out to be an old mate of mine from my Sunday football days and we had a good old natter and a catch up. I couldn't help thinking that the bloke had done pretty well for himself. Manchester United's new striker Andy Cole was due to perform the official opening and everybody was disappointed when he didn't show up and sent the young Neville brothers instead. Gary and Phil had only played a handful of games for United between them and Phil seemed a little shy and spent most of the afternoon in the background chatting with fans. In contrast Gary, as we would later come to expect, had plenty to say for himself, he was confident, assured, knowledgeable and, above all, friendly. He told us about how nervous he was when he made his debut, saying "You had Schmeichel screaming at you, Steve Bruce telling you off, Mark Hughes giving you a clip round the ear for not spotting one of his runs and Eric Cantona giving you dirty looks, and all this before going in at half-time to face Alex Ferguson." It was a great insight into just what it takes to be a Manchester United player. When I got back to the station I told anyone who would listen that Gary Neville was an absolute credit to his parents and would go on to captain United one day.

I also interviewed Fergie during my time at Signal Cheshire and I was a bag of nerves just thinking about it. The great man seemed surly and cautious when I introduced myself and shook his hand, but that all changed once I had assured him that I was a lifelong red. "That's good," he said, "So many of the media in Manchester are City fans, it drives me mad." I was amazed that he cared about such things, but after that we got on famously and it turned out to be another memorable day and one to tell the grandkids about.

Neil Sedaka didn't exactly take the Pineapple in his stride when we talked him into joining us for a swift one after the interview. The moment he walked in, he went as white as a sheet, suddenly remembered he needed to be somewhere and legged it. He did, however, do a great interview and talked enthusiastically about all the great songs he wrote all those years ago in the Brill Building on Broadway. I only wish we'd had a piano in the studio.

Adam Faith came in to promote his new book and was very nice, as was Midge Ure who told a filthy story about Paula Yates that involved sweetcorn. Thankfully, he told the story off-air.

Bernard Manning was someone I was a bit nervous about talking to live on air for obvious reasons, but he was on his best behaviour. I even got him to tell my favourite Bernard Manning joke, one I'd heard him tell on the Comedians TV show some 20-odd years earlier. Younger readers won't get the joke, so let me just say that way back, before The Beatles, young men aspired to have a haircut just like the film star Tony Curtis. Over to Bernard: "Fella goes to the barbers and says, 'Give me a Tony Curtis.' The barber shaves all his hair off, the poor bloke looks like a billiard ball. 'You pillock,' shouts the customer, 'Don't you know who Tony Curtis is?' 'I should do,' says the barber. 'I've seen The King and I fourteen times.'" Still makes me laugh all these years later.

One day in December, with Christmas coming up, our desperate sales team booked me in to do a show from a shed in the centre of Stockport. The shed was half-heartedly done up to resemble Santa's Grotto, but it was a freezing cold, wet and windy December day, the shed had no heating and I was soon in a foul temper. The mood was certainly not helped by various members of the public knocking on the shed door asking the question: "How much are your sheds, mate?" The owner of the shed insisted on being interviewed because, after all, it was his shed and he'd let us use it for the day but, really, how many questions can you ask a bloke about his shed? "So, what sort of sheds do you do?" and "How long have you been in the shed business?" The day was saved when our sales manager Ian managed to cajole Leslie Grantham and Vicki Michelle, who were appearing in panto at the local theatre. to come over and say hello. Leslie had been getting a bit of bad press at the time but I found him extremely likeable and down-to-earth, and as for Vicky, well, it was love at first sight – well, it was for me, anyway. They both threw themselves with gusto into my handshake game, and with Leslie we were able to get to Mahatma Gandhi via Freddie Mercury and Lord Mountbatten whilst Vicki got us to President Kennedy via The Beatles and Elvis. Both Leslie and Vicki were a joy to be with, no hint of ego and up for a laugh.

Can't really say the same about John Inman, he came in because he was promoting his new book, but he was bad-tempered, arrogant and rude. Before he came into the studio his assistant had whispered to me, "Be careful, he's been on the gin all morning," so maybe that had something to do with it. He just didn't seem to get that the interview was for his benefit, not mine, I wasn't the one trying to sell a book, although he did cheer up a bit when I told him that I used to work at Burton's and could relate to his "I'm free" catchphrase. John had started out as a window dresser and, in my limited experience, all window dressers were as gay as a daffodil. I did mention to him that back in the day when homosexuality was still illegal, a window dressers' annual conference must have been a great place to meet like-minded folk. Sadly, he didn't seem to want to talk about that.

I think the best interview I ever did, and possibly my best ever radio show, was with the late, great Ken Dodd on Budget Day. This was not too long after Doddy had been cleared of cheating the tax man. In one studio, we had a very serious accountant advising listeners to invest their money in shares and ISAs, while in my studio Ken was on top form telling people to "hide it under the floorboards". A few days later, I got a lovely hand-written note from the man himself saying how much he had enjoyed the interview. A subsequent phone call from Ken reiterated how much the interview had tickled the great man. The following day I went to see my mum and, knowing that Ken Dodd was one of the very few comedians that she had any time for, I proudly told her about the show. I had barely finished my tale when she picked up the Manchester Evening News and showed me an advert that she had highlighted with her biro, Manchester Airport was advertising for cleaners and they were paying seven pounds an hour. "Our John," she pleaded, "I do wish you'd get yourself a proper job."

Then there was Jimmy Savile. After getting the boot from Radio One, he syndicated his "Jimmy Savile's Old Record Club" show to a number of commercial stations, including Signal in Stoke and Signal Cheshire. As part of the deal, he agreed to make one personal appearance a year, so he was booked in, along with me, to switch on the Stockport Christmas lights. He didn't want paying, but he would love a box of his favourite cigars. To paraphrase the old pervert, "as it happens" a box of his favourite cigars cost five hundred smackers. Over the years and well before he died, I often said that I thought Savile was weird, and not in a good way. At the reception in the Mayor's office, he was introduced to a colleague of mine. "Oh no, not another DJ taking money that should be mine," jingled Savile. My mate tried to explain that Savile wouldn't even get out of bed for the money that he was earning, but he had lost interest, he had given his usual response upon meeting a fellow disc jockey and now had nothing else to say. I observed him using the same technique to a nurse and a fireman on the same night. A few years later, on the Louis Theroux documentary, his former chauffeur said that Savile had "absolutely no personality" and I saw it for myself that night in Stockport.

Another much talked about interview that had nothing to do with me involved my mate Jon Keighren who was presenting our Saturday afternoon show. He had been sent out to do alive outside broadcast from a marquee on the site of a new housing development in Timperley which, bizarrely, was being launched by the least talented member of the Jackson family, La Toya. According to Jon, the interview was going nowhere, until she insisted on swapping seats and moved into the chair right next to Jon, and suddenly he felt a hand rubbing up and down against the inside of his thigh and La Toya was staring deep into his embarrassed eyes. La Toya Jackson was coming on to my mate Jon, who swiftly curtailed the interview and headed to the bar for a much-needed pint. As he tried to process what had just occurred, one of La Toya's burly minders approached Jon and said, "Miss Jackson has just opened a bottle of champagne in her suite and would love you to join her." The best that my mate could come up with was, "I'm sorry, I can't, I promised to go to my mum's for my tea."

The social side of life at Signal Cheshire was excellent, especially if, like me, you were single. At least once a week we would be invited to a record company 'meet and greet' where one of their artists would sing a couple of songs from their new album, shake everybody's hand and, of course, hope their latest offering would get played on the radio. It was strange how quickly the place emptied when they started charging for the drinks. One such night the 'meet and greet' revolved around Lulu, and the record company was being exceptionally generous with the wine. A few of us from Signal got talking to Lulu and she seemed like great fun. I was crossing my fingers that none of my by now tipsy work mates would let on about one of my standard jokes. I used to say that Lulu had it written into her contract that whenever she appeared on a TV or radio show that the host had to begin the interview by saying something like "Lulu, you look marvellous, how on earth do you do it?" Thankfully, they all behaved themselves, unlike me, who, fuelled by too many glasses of free vino, had the audacity to ask Lulu to dance. The DJ had started to play the brilliant Edwyn Collins song

"A Girl Like You" and I said to Lulu, "Oh, Lulu, I love this record, do you fancy a dance?" Well, the look she gave me would have turned many a lesser, or at least a more sober man to stone. She turned on her delicate heel and flounced off. I was able to remind her of the incident when we met again ten years later.

One evening after my show Neil Cossar took me to The Pineapple and dropped an absolute bombshell. He was resigning. I couldn't believe it, Neil seemed happy in the job and everybody loved working for him. but it turned out that he had been getting a bit of stick from one or two of the directors and he'd had enough. Signal Cheshire was by now a very successful radio station with good figures and a great line up but no matter how hard we tried we could not shift Key 103, formerly Piccadilly Radio, off the number one spot. If we ever started to get close, they would just throw a load of money at it, whether it was giving away a car or a holiday or shed loads of cash. We just couldn't live with their spending power, so when Neil left it was decided to advertise for a new Programme Controller.

I sussed out the new guy the moment he walked through the door and opened his mouth. He might as well have had "bullshitter" engraved on his forehead. He name-dropped for England. How he gave such-and-such his big chance in radio, how his previous employers had thanked him for saving their station and how he planned to bring some big names to Signal Cheshire. He knew everybody who was anybody in radio, and they were all keen to work for him, or so he said. I couldn't help but wonder how this broadcasting genius had ended up in this little radio station in Stockport. He made no secret of the fact that he thought all the presenters on the station needed replacing, and he seemed to be looking at me as he said it. My opinion of him was mirrored by his of me, the question was: who would blink first? A few of my colleagues started looking for new jobs right away, but I decided that, because he was such an obvious fraud, he would be gone before me, but I was wrong. Most Fridays he would leave at lunchtime, so he could be home with his family in London for the weekend, but this particular Friday he was still stinking the place out at 6pm when I finished my show. When he beckoned me into his office, I knew full well what was coming. To be honest, when the bullet was fired it was a relief, because the previous few months had been soul destroying, not just for me but for everyone at the station. Apparently, he had to persuade the directors to get rid of me, promising them that he would bring in somebody who would double the audience. I was given a £1000 pay-off and I offered to bet him that thousand pounds that nobody would ever come close to my listening figures in the afternoon. He didn't answer, just smirked. Less than a year later, he was gone, after halving the audience and going through at least a dozen presenters, none of whom were household names and, frankly, none of them were any good. Meanwhile I was out of work and applying for jobs. By this time Marc had come to live with me, Elaine had got herself a new boyfriend, a supercilious New Zealander called Ken, who Marc hated, and I got the impression that the feeling was mutual. When Marc confided in me that Ken was a bully who made him go to bed at seven o'clock at night (Marc was 14 years old at this stage) I decided enough was enough and he should come and live with me. I got home from work one evening to find the New Zealander chucking Marc's belongings onto my driveway. The moment he saw me he tried to jump in his car, but I grabbed him by the neck and threatened to strangle him. Ken was a lot taller and quite a bit younger and stronger than me, but I was angrier than I'd ever been in my life. For years I had tortured myself for deserting Marc when I did. I had been a lousy father, but I was determined to put it right. I'm proud to say that Marc went from being a moody teenager to a polite and decent young man and when he became the first Owen to go to university I was bursting with pride.

I have to say during my time at Signal Cheshire it was a pleasure to really get to know Craig Cash, a genuinely down-to-earth funny guy. We had our disagreements from time to time, because he was never afraid to speak up if he thought you were behaving like a prat. Craig presented a unique radio show three nights a week playing underground music and songs from the Indie charts. He would spend hours ploughing through demo tapes that unknown singers and bands had sent in to him. We used to wind him up about it, but he would say, "One of these days I'll get a tape from the new Beatles and I don't want to miss it." One lunchtime in the Pineapple, I was approached by a bloke in overalls who handed me a cassette and said, "These are two lads who work with me on the building site, they have a group and they are pretty good." When I got back to Signal, there was Craig, as usual, knee deep in cassettes, so I casually chucked him the new one and said, "There you go, Cashy, have a listen, you never know it could be the new Beatles." The two lads on the tape turned out to be Oasis. We were all aware that Craig was a very good comedy writer because at the time he was already working with Caroline Aherne, but none of us had any idea he would go on to have the blockbusting success he did with "The Royle Family" and later "Early Doors". It really couldn't have happened to a nicer guy.

Before we move on from Signal Cheshire, I'd like to give special thanks to a girl called Jackie O'Malley. Jackie was the office receptionist, but I soon recognised that she had a real talent for radio and would become a regular feature on my show. She is a sparky Irish redhead and we bounced off each other brilliantly. She always gave as good, if not better, than she got. Some of the best things I ever did on the radio involved Jackie and I owe her a big thank you. When I listen to some of today's breakfast show double-headers, I know immediately when two people have been thrown together and it's painful for both of them, not to mention the long-suffering listener. Me and Jackie hit it off the moment the "on air" light went on. I might get slaughtered for saying this but, by and large, I am not a fan of women presenters on the radio, although Sarah Cox on Radio 2 is an exception, but Jackie was different class.

CHAPTER 14: "New Kid in Town", The Eagles 1977 (Number 20)

After getting the bullet from Signal Cheshire, I disappeared down a black hole for a while. Apart from the final six months, I really loved my time in Stockport. I made some great friends and it was the happiest time of my life. On one hand, it felt like unfinished business and that I still had plenty in the tank where radio was concerned, on the other hand I really didn't feel up to going to another station and having to prove myself all over again. It was alien to me, but essentially I was depressed and feeling sorry for myself, until I got another phone call from John Evington, who told me that everybody in Stoke had been opposed to me losing my job, but that the "bullshitter" had been adamant (although John was far too polite to use that word). With the new football season about to start he said he was looking for somebody to present the Saturday afternoon football show. He explained that in all the years that Signal had been on the air they had not been able to make any kind of impact on the local BBC station's audience figures. It seemed that people who listened to Signal all day, every day would automatically switch over to BBC Radio Stoke for their Saturday football fix. John had decided to give the show one last chance and he wanted me to sort it out. So, on the 31st of August 1997, a date that would in a few hours become incredibly significant, I sat down to present the football show on Signal 2 on the medium wave band. It wasn't long before I began to wish I'd never bothered. A couple of days beforehand I had travelled to Stoke to have a look round the studio and everything seemed pretty straightforward. The one thing that the station engineer failed to point out to me was how the complex "talk-back" system worked and, to be honest, it never occurred to me to ask, so what happened on that first Saturday was just as much my fault as theirs. The problem was this: while the reporters at the ground could hear me, I couldn't hear them, which was a major setback, but not the only one I would encounter on that fraught afternoon. As I would later find out, Signal sound engineers were never to be found at the weekend. We should have had reporters at each of our local clubs, Port Vale, Crewe Alexandra and, of course, Stoke City. Stoke were away in London and, as three o'clock approached, I was becoming increasingly worried that the Stoke reporter had not checked in. This, as well as no talk-back, was the last thing I needed. At about ten minutes to three the phone rang: "I've been driving round for an hour and there's nowhere to park," said the reporter. "This is useless, I'm off home!" There may have been a few expletives in that call as well, but the long and the short of it was that our intrepid Stoke City reporter had thrown his dummy out of the pram and was past caring. I desperately tried to reason with him, reminding him of the possible consequences of such an action, but his mind was made up. I must admit that my concern was more for me than him, this was my very first show and it was going tits up in the grandest of fashions. I was yet to meet Signal's Head of Sport Simon Humphreys, but I had been told that, although he was a decent bloke, he didn't suffer fools. By half-time on that August afternoon, he must have come to the conclusion that I was the biggest numbskull on the planet, and we had a blazing row on the telephone. Just when I thought the worst afternoon of my career was coming to an end, I got a call from the bloke who was due to present the show after me saying he was not feeling well, and could I cover for him. It's probably the one time I really *didn't* feel like doing a radio show. As I drove back to Manchester at well past ten o'clock on that Saturday night with a splitting headache, I tuned into Radio 5 to listen to the late, great Patty Caldwell, when suddenly she announced that Princess Diana had been involved in a car crash in Paris and was seriously ill in hospital. The following morning, I got up, turned the television on and the newsreader was wearing a black tie, and I knew right away what that meant. I shouted upstairs to Marc who was still in bed that Princess Di was dead. He rushed downstairs and we watched the gruesome story unfold in total silence.

I would have loved to have been a fly on the wall of John Evington's office on the Monday morning because I was later told that there was a queue of people lining up to tell him that I was hopeless and would have to go. Whether or not John didn't take kindly to having people telling him who he should or shouldn't employ, or whether he was just too busy dealing with the Princess Diana situation, I'll never know, but thankfully he dug his heels in and let me get on with it. 99 out of one hundred programme controllers would have gone for the easy option, but I'm forever grateful to John for sticking by me, especially when you consider the long and fairly successful career I went on to enjoy at Signal 2.

Left to my own devices, the football show started to find an identity and I was able to incorporate many of my own ideas and competitions which, slowly but surely, improved the listening figures. This was helped enormously by the introduction of "The Friday Football Show" hosted by myself and a local commentator called George Andrews. George was a bit of a legend in the Staffordshire area, a total eccentric who a lot of people tended to write off as a bit of a nutcase, but he knew his football and he had a little black book that contained the names of everybody who was anybody in the great game. That little black book proved to be invaluable, as our Friday show quickly became a must-listen-to show for anybody who loved footie. Despite the fact that the BBC local radio station had a similar show that went out at the same time, and they paid their guests up to a hundred pounds to appear, local footballing legends much preferred to come on our show because, whereas the Beeb's output was carefully scripted, ours was totally ad-hoc and a free for all, an absolute laugh-a-minute, and all our guests received in return for their time and trouble was a couple of glasses of white wine, which, of course, tended to relax them and loosen their tongue a little bit. George and I used to argue like hell during almost every show and some people thought it was all a bit of an act but it was nothing of the sort. During one programme I thought he was talking so much rubbish that I turned his mic off, but it didn't stop him from still trying to get his point across. Like I said, George was a law unto himself and sometimes he would leave you absolutely speechless at some of the things he came out with. For instance, one Saturday afternoon he was commentating on a snow-affected Crewe Alexandra game and I went over to him for a pre-match scene-setter. "Welcome to a very icy Gresty Road," said George, "where all the players have been out on the pitch trying out different types of underwear." He meant footwear, of course, but that was Georgie Boy, on another planet.

I cherish the memories of those football shows, especially the Friday one, because I got to meet and become friends with some genuine legends both locally and nationally. People with great stories to tell, such as Alan Hudson, Adrian Heath, George Eastham, Jimmy Greenhoff, Bill Bentley, Dennis Smith, Mike Pejic, Lou Macari, as well as household names such as Tommy Docherty, Nobby Stiles and Gordon Banks. I was especially pleased with myself when I introduced Gordon by saying something like: "Our Friday football show is one for the dads and the lads, so lads ask your dad about Gordon Banks, the greatest goalie who ever played the game. Back in 1970 in the World Cup in Mexico the Germans were so frightened of Gordon's ability that they put something despicable in his pre-match cup of tea and he spent the entire game stuck in the toilet doubled up in agonising pain while England went out of the tournament." With that, I turned to Gordon and said: "Are you OK now, Gordon, or would you like to go before we start?" Thankfully, the great man thought it was hilarious - well, he smiled, at least. One Friday night show in particular sticks in my mind, our guest was the mercurial former Chelsea and Stoke City legend Alan Hudson and the topic was memorable terrace chants. A Celtic fan phoned in and told us about the time his team signed a French player who gloried in the name of Rafael Scheidt, who made his debut against Hibernian. The poor bloke was having a bit of a nightmare and it wasn't long before the Hibs fans started chanting: "You're Rafael, and you know you are!" Huddy said his favourite was the one away fans sang at former West Ham striker Bobby Zamora, to the tune of Dean Martin's That's Amore, it went like this: "When you're sat in row z and the ball hits your head - that's Zamora!" That was our Friday football show in a nutshell, irreverent, edgy and bloody funny.

One day I got another call from John Evington asking me if I fancied taking over the Signal 2 evening show, eight till midnight, Monday to Friday.

"Has Judith Chalmers got a passport?" was my reply

"Sorry?"

"Is the Pope a Catholic?"

"Is that a yes?"

"Yes! Yes! Yes! I would love to give it a go!" At a subsequent meeting (and people who have ever worked for John Evington will find this hard to believe) he paid me a compliment. He said: "Some presenters are holders, some are keepers and some are builders. You are all three, which is rare." I had to ask him what he meant, so he explained that some people can hold the audience they inherit, some can keep that audience and some can build on that audience. Now, like me, you might think that at least two of those descriptions boil down to pretty much the same thing, but as a compliment from John Evington was about as rare as rocking horse droppings, I wasn't about to argue. John told me that, once again, I would be taking over a show that was struggling for listeners and that I had my work cut out. That didn't faze me one bit, and I threw myself and everything I had into that show, after 10pm especially when I tried to create a late-night programme in which everybody could get involved, a kind of secret society that was to become less and less of a secret as time went on. I tore up the music log and played some fantastic songs that you just never hear on the radio, as well as a few 'Junior Choice'-type classics that people of a certain age might remember 'Stewpot' playing all those years ago. Songs like "My Brother" by Terry Scott and "Three Wheels on my Wagon" by the New Christy Minstrels. I heard that pub landlords were turning off the jukebox at ten o'clock to let everybody join in with the trivia questions I was setting, and people even phoned to say they no longer bothered with the telly in the evening because they preferred to listen to me. I took that as the greatest compliment of all, because, as much as I love radio, I would never really dream of turning the television off at night to listen to it. To be honest, there didn't seem to be anybody out there doing anything interesting on the radio, anyway. Just the same old songs, the same old bored-sounding jocks, all hoping that a daytime gig was just around the corner.

After about a year, the listening figures had gone up tenfold, and I was

doing better than some of the daytime output, which is totally unheard of. It's a show I remain incredibly proud of to this day. I remember the very first phone call I got on that very first evening show – it was from a lady called Anthea, and it went something like this:
"Hello, Signal 2?"
"So we're stuck with you now, are we?"
"Pardon?"
"Are you here for good now?"
"Er, I think so."
"Well, I don't think much of you and I don't think anyone else round here will either. Are you the best they could find?" The phone went dead. Thanks, Anthea, just the tonic I needed to calm my first night nerves. I have to say though, Anthea did become a big fan and would phone me several times during my shows. When I later moved on to the breakfast show, me and Anthea developed a routine that was played out the day before I went away on holiday. Having mentioned that I got the Delhi-belly the moment I set foot on foreign soil, we would re-enact the sketch from the Les Dawson show, in which Les, dressed as the gossiping old lady Cissie and her friend Ada, played by Roy Barrowclough, discussed Cissie's recent holiday in Greece.

Ada (Anthea): "Did you see the Acropolis?"
Cissie (Me): "See it? I was never off it!" Well, it made us laugh, anyway.

Talking of Les Dawson, Anthea came up with a phrase I'd never heard before, but I thought it was one of the funniest things I'd ever heard. She said: "I do like Les Dawson, but he's got a face like a dropped pie." A face like a dropped pie! Oscar Wilde would have been proud of that.

Another regular caller was Jo, who also became a much-loved part of the show. She always gave me the impression that she was struggling for money, but she was always happy and cheerful. One time I hadn't heard from her for a couple of weeks and was getting a bit worried when out of the blue she rang up saying she was sorry she hadn't been in touch, but she had a new boyfriend and he'd been moving in. It was the first I'd heard of a boyfriend, so I said: "Blimey, Jo, you're a dark horse." She told me that she'd known this bloke for years and he had once shared a prison cell with her ex hubby, "but he's going straight now," she said. "They all say that" was my reply. She then said that this new boyfriend had been studying Buddhism in Nepal. "Are you sure he hasn't been doing a stretch in Strangeways?" I said, only half joking. Jo continued: "No, I've seen all the photos, the monks gave him the name 'The One Who Smiles at the Sun' - but I just call him Kev." Brilliant! I was devastated when I heard that Jo had suddenly passed away as she was only in her forties, such a shame.

Another memorable call on that eventful first night came when, for some reason, I got onto the subject of the cult 70s TV show "Monkey". If you remember, it was a badly-dubbed Japanese programme that featured kung fu, talking fish and a variety of weird and not so wonderful creatures. I said: "Ring now if you can remember the names of any of the characters in the TV show Monkey." The phones lit up and I answered right away.
"Dave Dee Dozy Beaky Mick and Tich," said the caller.
"What are you talking about?"
"Dave Dee Dozy Beaky Mick and Tich" he shouted. "They were The Monkees!" I'm still trying to work that one out all these years later. And to think my mum once said to me: "Sitting around for hours, playing records, don't you ever get bored?"

When the new programme controller, Kevin Howard, offered me the breakfast show, I gratefully snapped his hand off, even though I certainly didn't consider myself a morning person and I was still living in Manchester at the time, which meant getting up in the middle of the night. But when you are offered breakfast on radio you simply don't say no. It's the Crown Jewel. I loved working for Kevin, he was a superb bloke and, I have to say, he seemed to love my show, which of course filled me with confidence. John Evington had moved upstairs and while everybody respected John it seemed like all the windows had been opened and a breath of fine fresh air had swept through the building when Kevin took over the day-to-day running of both Signal One and Signal Two. Signal One was the hot FM station catering for the under-35 audience, and all the budget was dedicated to that station and, to be honest, John sometimes seemed to be all-consumed with what was happening on Signal One. The guys on Two felt a bit disillusioned and ignored, but that all changed when Kev took over. I started on the breakfast show on the 15th of October 2002 (that date again).

Getting up at four in the morning to drive to Stoke certainly took a bit of getting used to. One time I woke up and the clock said ten past five, the alarm hadn't gone off and I was on air at six! I jumped in the car and headed off, but I was a little curious to see quite a few house lights were on already and there seemed to be more people than usual on the streets. To be honest, there were usually no lights on and nobody on the roads, but it wasn't until I reached the main road that it hit me. It was the rush hour. I had gone for a kip in the afternoon and woken up, not at ten past five in the morning, but at ten past five in the evening. On another occasion I jumped in the car and started the engine but the car refused to move. I got out to have a look and the bloody thing was on bricks, somebody had sneaked onto the drive in the middle of the night and nicked all four tyres.

Did I mention that Droylsden in Manchester had more than its fair share of work-shy layabouts? What followed was a frantic taxi ride to the railway station just in time to catch the 5am train.

After a few months of travelling up and down the M6 I decided to buy a house nearer the radio station and, because I still wanted to be able to go and see my mum once a week, I thought Crewe might be a better option than Stoke-on-Trent. Once I'd settled in Crewe, I felt a lot less fatigued and a lot more able to really get to grips with making the breakfast show a success. One of the first things I did was introduce the dysfunctional radio family "The Bradshaw's" into the programme. At a meeting Kevin was, as usual, very supportive, but John Evington less so, in fact he told me that The Bradshaw's would go down like a lead balloon, mainly because it was set in Manchester and the people in the Stoke-on-Trent area were quite parochial. If you are not familiar with the series, The Bradshaw's consists of Alf, the domineering father, his long-suffering wife Audrey, who suffers from a Mrs Malaprop syndrome ("Hell has no fury like a woman's corns") and their seven-year-old son Billy. Set in the 1960s in a little terraced house, very similar to the one I grew up in, The Bradshaw's struck a chord with me right away because, for one thing, Alf could have been my old man. By the way, I take no credit for the idea, I first heard the series some 30 years earlier on Phil Wood's brilliant show on Piccadilly Radio, but as the saying goes, if you want a new idea look in an old book. The Bradshaw's were the creation of a man called Buzz Hawkins who I later discovered was about the same age as me and lived just up the road. I'm amazed that we never met as kids, as he went to the local Catholic school St Brigit's, the sworn enemy of Grange Street Secondary Modern. Buzz seamlessly did all three voices on the show - I say 'did', in fact he still does. To this day, Buzz performs his sell-out shows up and down the country. The idea did meet with a few negative comments early on, but soon pretty much everyone became a fan and when we did the live shows at the local theatre the place was packed and the atmosphere electric. After a few months John Evington did admit that I was right and he was wrong, another first. All radio shows aspire to be famous for one thing and mine became synonymous with The Bradshaws. Here's one of my favourite exchanges between Billy and his mother:

Billy (rushing in from school): "Mam, what's a general erection?"

Audrey (flustered): "Ooh, er, ask your father."

"Have I got one?"

"Not until you're 21, Billy love."

One of the best things I did on the show was cajoling the station producer Chris Peace into helping me write some comedy songs and jingles. I would come up with the words and Chris, being a trained musician, would turn them into a catchy tune. Kevin Howard suggested we write a Christmas song, with all the proceeds going to our "Help a Signal Child" charity. A few days later, I had written the words to "Father Christmas Stole My Girl" and Chris, as usual, rose to the occasion and turned it into a brilliant sing-along Christmas single. We ended up selling over 3,000 copies from our reception alone and raised an awful lot of money.

One show in particular sticks in my mind. It was the 8th of August, the anniversary of the Great Train Robbery, so I decided that me and the listeners would form our own gang of villains to pull off the crime of the century. I asked for volunteers and the phones went crazy. A taxi driver offered to drive our getaway car and a cobbler working at the local branch of Timpson's said he was just the man if we wanted any keys cutting. By the way, as Harry Hill once said, "Why are cobblers so good at cutting keys?" A solicitor even offered to defend us should we get caught, three or four lady listeners volunteered to become "gangster's molls" to keep the blokes amused in their hide out as they waited for the dust to settle. Dedicated fan of the show George Jackson, who played for Stoke City in the 70s but was now the owner of one of the many pot banks in the area, offered to help us finance the heist. George was just one of the many people who started off being just a voice on the end of the phone but ended up becoming a very good friend. On that show I nicknamed him China George, as in china and pottery, and these days he is known to everybody by that name. So, on that particular morning while all the other breakfast shows were talking about the new release from Will Young or reading out bits of trivia from the Daily Star, we were creating top quality audience participation radio. I later learned that the show was played back to a seminar of programme controllers as an example of going that extra mile. And I have still never won a Sony Award!

CHAPTER 15: "Love of My Life", The Dooleys 1977 (Number 9)

One of my mates, I think it may have been Jon, came up with the idea of a Signal Cheshire reunion week in Lanzarote combined with a golfing holiday. I had briefly taken up golf some years earlier, but it really brought out the worst in me, I would end up chucking my clubs all over the course in total frustration. What an annoying game. One week you think you are getting the hang of it, but the next you are completely shying the ball all over the place, so I said I'd skip the golf, but I was definitely up for the week in Lanzarote.

While the rest of the gang played 18 holes, I would catch up on a bit of sleep by the pool. The holiday was a riotous success, an absolute laugh-a-minute, and it would for many years become an annual thing, until that is, the inevitable happened, people started getting married and having kids. It was on that first holiday in Lanzarote I was able to astound the gang with my karaoke performances. I only ever did one song: "Why Must I Be a Teenager in Love" but I did it in a style I imagined that Elvis would have adopted to perform it. I don't think it's an exaggeration to say that I always brought the house down and it became a much-requested staple of all future get togethers.

One holiday in particular sticks in my mind, it was in Malaga and we had noticed a quirky little bistro at the end of the road, so one day I strolled down intending to borrow a menu to take back to the gang. I entered the tiny building and it was dark and closed, chairs on the tables and all that. Suddenly an older woman appeared from the kitchen and I started to explain that there was a group of us staying at a nearby villa and could I borrow a menu. She stopped me in mid-sentence and started shouting, "No English, No English." I said "What? You don't serve English people?" Once again all I got was, "No English, No English." I turned on my heel and stormed out, I couldn't wait to tell the lads about this grotty little racist bistro, when a bloke started shouting from behind and he was English. I blurted out my disgust and he shook his head. He explained that the lady was trying to tell me that she didn't *speak* English, of course they served English people! He was the owner, a Londoner, and I started to get that salted snail feeling all over again. We ended up eating there that very night and were all in agreement that it was the best food we had ever tasted, even the frogs' legs which, of course, tasted like chicken.

Our last holiday in Majorca was sadly a bit of a disaster, the fridge/freezer wasn't working properly and every one of us got a bit of food poisoning, especially Rick the Scouser who got a really bad dose. In

Hello Hello .. A day out at Belle Vue Amusement Park . The closest Mancunians ever got to Disneyland.

Grange Street Secondary Modern (hopeless 3rd year football team. That's me front row second left.

Number 7 Moody Street Bradford Manchester . no bathroom or running hot water and the toilet in the back yard. On the corner is my dad's local The Duke of Edinburgh pub. notice a lack of TV Ariel's.

On holiday at Squires Gate Holiday Camp near Blackpool .. Is that a gun in my pocket . . . or a packet of Spangles ?

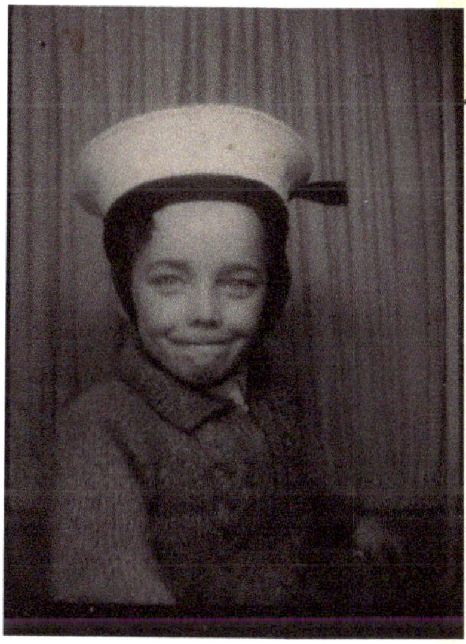

This is me joining up. All the nice girls love a Sailor, but I think I must have lied about my age

Bradford Memorial Junior School . I'm the stern looking young fellow in the middle of the front row

A World of His Own

Ethelred Longstream was a boy, his parents were inordinantly rich and he was given everything he wanted.

He never went playing with other children of his age (Ethelred was ten years old), he had a private school teacher who came every morning to be almost driven out of her mind by Ethelred's incessant dreaming. It is on one of these such occasions that we join him now.

"Once long ago Androcles had to fight a lion to . . . . ", the teacher was reading to Ethelred out of a book entitled "Androcles and the Friendly Lion", when Master Longstream fell into a deep, deep dream.

"There he is Ethelrocles, quickly after him."
Ethelrocles had escaped the clutches of seventeen lions; he had counted them as he chopped off their heads; but now he was being pursued by Roman soldiers. Ethelred galloped swiftly up Mount Asbillmiddleah the largest mountain in Spasmadica, and picked up a two ton boulder and threw it at the fifty one soldiers, he counted them as he galloped up Mount Asbillmiddleah.

"Well thats the Roman soldiers gone," thought Ethelred. "Uh. What's this?" Ethelred had noticed Persian soldiers on horseback. He had escaped from them after being put in the death cell for robbing Mrs Butterworth's sweet shop of all the jelly babies in stock.

"Look," cried a soldier,"there he is, there's Fred upon that mountain," (a steady improvement in names don't you think?) as Ethelred raced down the mountain he tripped over a boulder. The soldiers charged on the bemused Ethelred. The Persian leader drew his sword ready to thrust it into the body of the frightened boy when, "Now Ethelred I would like you to write me an essay about Androcles."

"Saved " exclaimed Ethelred as the teacher glared at him in annoyance.

John Owen.

My contribution to the school magazine. At 13 years old I was into writing stories. poems and saving the World.

In Santa's Grotto with "Dirty Den" and Vicki Michelle. Actually Santa's Grotto was a garden shed in the middle of Stockport Town Centre.

A Signal Cheshire fancy dress day. For the life of me I can't remember the reason for it, but by this time we had retired to the sanctuary of The Pineapple. I also have no idea how Eric Idle managed to gate crash the party.

Tiffanys Manchester circa 1976. Posing before closing

Signal Cheshire double header on the afternoon show with the fiery red head Jackie O'Malley. Who always gave as good as she got. If not better. We did some terrific shows together.

Concentration levels high as I change a nappy.

1984 Marc in his jimjams. Me dolled up for some reason.

Adam Faith called in to promote his new book

Putting in a gruelling 2 hour shift on Hitmix Radio

Mum with Marc. She was never happier

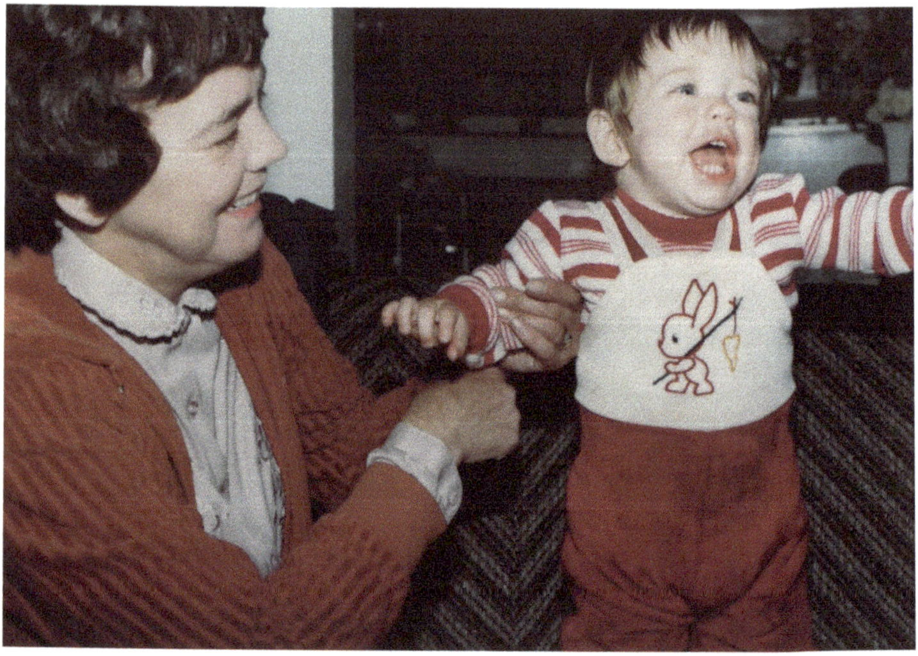

On holiday in Majorca with 3 year old Marc 1984.

Meeting the great man. Nervous as a kitten...

Lynn and I for my son Marc's wedding in Dublin. All very emotional

Messing about at Jilly's night club in Manchester (circa72) that hairstyle was all the go at the time

With Buzz Hawkins ..the genius behind The Bradshaw's.

Chucking it down at Disneyland with an Earthquake heading our way. But we kept going. Me and Shawn Tilley a great experience.

The Signal Cheshire fancy dress party. Still no idea what the reason was . And no idea who the bloke at the back is.

Proud Dad with son Marc on Sydney Harbour Bridge

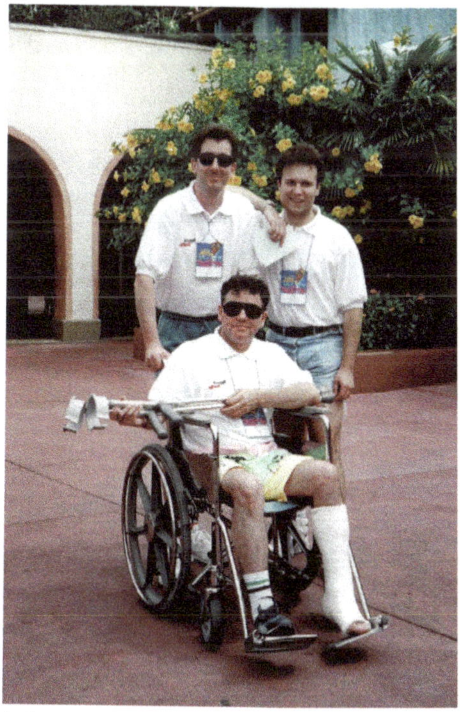

In Orlando with fellow presenter Shawn Tilley and Producer Neil Cossar .A broken leg was not going to keep me from a freebie at Disneyland ..businessclass

Me, Jackie O'Malley and Breakfast Show presenter Dave Stearn opening a bottle to celebrate great listening figures on Signal Cheshire

addition, he was suffering from toothache which made it a miserable time for him. I put my lifelong dislike of Scousers to one side in the case of Rick, who was a terrific guy, absolutely one of the lads. One day we were all messing about with a beach ball in the swimming pool as we listened to the golfers wrestling with their game on the other side of the fence. The only person not in the pool was, of course, Rick who was huddled in a poolside chair with a blanket round him feeling very sorry for himself. The ball went out of the pool and landed twenty or so yards from where Rick was nursing his wounds. Well, the unsympathetic cry went up, "Come on, Rick, you lazy bastard, get off your arse and get the ball." Rick staggered from his seat and made his way unsteadily towards the ball, suddenly he went down like he'd been shot, flat out, lifeless. It turns out that a miscued golf ball had flown into our villa, shot straight across the pool and hit poor Rick square on the temple. It just wasn't his week.

By the way, talking of people getting married, I think it's about time I introduced you to the woman who would become the love of my life and my second wife. I was in a hotel bar with the rest of the Signal Two crew celebrating excellent quarterly listening figures and Lynn was enjoying an office party with a group of her colleagues. We had both had a few glasses of wine so, stoked up with Dutch courage, we got chatting and I invited her for a meal the following week, which she surprisingly accepted. I must say that prior to meeting Lynn, I thought I was having the time of my life, enjoying my job, coming and going as I pleased with nobody to answer to. In reality, I was drinking far too much and existing on ready meals and toasties. Lynn got me off the whisky and started giving me proper home-cooked meals.

Fairly early in our relationship we went on holiday to Spain and I think it helped convince both of us that we had met our life partners. Lynn and I went on quite a few memorable holidays after that and we came up with a game that would become a staple part of our week away: "Lookie-Likies", seeking out holidaymakers who were the double of famous people. Over the year we saw Richard Branson in a restaurant in Ibiza, Roman Abramovich strolling down the beach in Portugal and the absolute spit of Cliff Richard in the hotel bar in Minorca. My absolute favourite was the former England manager Fabio Capello who, to our amazement, was working behind the counter in a supermarket in Zante. It kept us amused for hours.

We got married in a low-key ceremony on the glorious 12th of August 2016 and had a wedding breakfast at Frankie and Benny's in Crewe. A bit different to Marc who married his beautiful Jacquie in a Downton Abbey-style castle in Dublin just a few days later. I was so proud and emotional that day I cried like a big baby, especially when the vicar informed everyone that the candle on the altar had been requested by Marc in memory of his beloved Nana who "couldn't be here today". It was a wonderful gesture and once again the floodgates opened. Mum would have been bursting with pride.

When Marc first announced that he was going to emigrate to Australia, I was remarkably chilled about the whole idea. I assumed he'd stay there for a few months and then return with his tail between his legs because that's what would have happened if it had been me. I would have struggled to make friends, been terribly lonely and my new life would have become a nightmare. However, I misjudged my son, he's far more confident and outgoing than me, he can talk to anyone and be at home in anyone's company. For me it's that 'talking to myself in a darkened room' thing again. I think Marc must get his gregarious confidence from his mum, because he certainly doesn't get it from me. He has been in Australia for over 15 years now and built a wonderful life for himself. He lives in a beautiful apartment overlooking the beach with his gorgeous wife and little boy and runs his own recruitment company that he's built up from scratch. I could not be prouder.

I'm also glad that my mum was able to meet Lynn before she died because she was always saying that she wished I could settle down and get married and she really got on well with Lynn. It all started to go downhill with mum when she had an operation for a kidney tumour, although she seemed to recover from that, she lost loads of weight and was down to about five stone when she died. She'd started having lots of falls and broken bones while living in Manchester, but the final straw was when she answered the phone one afternoon to what we think must have been a cold caller. Because she was very deaf, she always had the telly on full blast, and she had asked the caller to hold on while she turned the television down. She tripped over the coffee table and broke her hip, the poor thing lay there in agony all night until she was rescued at dawn by the milkman. I decided enough was enough and she had to come and live near me.

We found a perfect bungalow just round the corner that she was able to move right into and I paid for it until she could sell her own house in Manchester, which meant that I could call in and see her two or three times a day to make her a meal and have a little chat and at least she had a couple of happier years before she passed away. I only wish I'd had the idea for this book while she was still alive because, although she struggled to remember what happened last week, remembering the events of 50 years ago were a doddle. God bless the old girl, I never really appreciated her until it was too late. Actually, that's not true, I did very much appreciate her, but took her for granted I suppose. I genuinely assumed that she would see us all out.

Spurred on by the success of our Christmas record in 2006, I had the idea of writing a World Cup song. Once again, I wrote the words and Chris turned it into a great tune. "Starting Together" was again only really intended to be played on my breakfast show but it was so damn catchy that every presenter on the two stations insisted on playing it. Initially, once again, we were only selling it on our reception and at roadshows, but it seemed like everybody wanted a copy. One day the manager of the local HMV record store telephoned Kevin Howard to ask about the song - apparently they too had been inundated with requests for a copy. I did CD signings in the store that attracted really long queues, in fact one chap told me that the previous week he had travelled to the Trafford Centre in Manchester to get a signed copy of Pele's new book and the queue was not a patch on ours!

The song was selling so many copies in that HMV store that we found ourselves at number two in the Indie charts, and then in June 2006 I picked up a copy of Music Week magazine and there we were in the top 40. We entered the charts just above Paul Simon and just below Madonna. The people who compiled the charts rang Kevin Howard wanting to know what was going on because they just could not believe that a song could enter the top 40 from sales in just one shop. I sat back and waited for a record company to notice what was going on and inviting us to sign a contract, but nothing. Eventually I started ringing them only to be told that they all had their own World Cup song to promote, so had no time for ours. To this day I still think the record companies missed a trick because I firmly believe that "Standing Together" was the third best football song ever, just behind Three Lions and World in Motion. With professional promotion and a proper record label, the song would definitely have been a smash hit and its inclusion on compilation albums would have meant that me and Chris would have been made for life. As it was the "Help a Signal Child" charity got another big windfall.

I remember Marc telling me that he was in a bar in Manchester one Saturday night and a group of girls from Stoke-on-Trent were singing the song at the top of their voices. Marc went over and said: "My Dad wrote that song!" Yes, of course he did, now get lost. There are a few lines in the song that I'm particularly proud of, delivered by me with suitable pathos:

"In our smoky front room, just me and my dad,
The best fun together that we ever had,
Singing and dancing and I don't know how,
But I sense that he's with me now...

Standing Together we'll conquer the world,
Standing Together every man boy and girl,
You know we're right behind you."
Still brings a lump to my throat.

One of my holiday reunion buddies, Ed James, who, after leaving Signal Cheshire, has gone on to have a stellar career as the breakfast show presenter on Heart FM in Birmingham, had a birthday coming up and his girlfriend suggested a surprise party. So, one Saturday evening after the football show, we headed off to the Radisson Hotel in Brum. The night was going very well, old friends in abundance, people chatting over a glass of wine or a pint of lager, it was all very sensible, until somebody shouted, "Let's go on the shots"! The next thing I remember is waking up at five o'clock on the Sunday morning and not having a clue where I was. On rubbing my eyes, I was greeted by what looked like a scene from one of those Cecil B. DeMille biblical orgies. A roomful of near-naked dolly birds dancing with sozzled well-dressed middle-aged men. Where was I? How did I get here? Had I died and gone to heaven? Or was this indeed the bowels of hell? I wondered off to seek a friendly face and immediately bumped into my mate Jon who informed me that I was in fact in Birmingham's number one lap dancing establishment. Apparently, I'd fallen asleep the minute we entered the place and missed all the fun. It was an old trick of mine, every year I would go to the Signal Christmas Party but fall fast asleep when it got to about nine o'clock at night.

Talking of Christmas, I was meandering round Manchester on the Saturday before Christmas and I found myself in Shudehill, the Jewish quarter of the city. I was just indulging in a harmless bit of window shopping when I noticed a tiny jeweller's shop I had never seen before. To be honest, blink and you'd miss it. In the window was a watch, an absolute belter. I've always had a thing about watches, so I marched straight in, completely ignoring my life long maxim "Never go into a shop that does not display its prices in the window". I had a price in mind, eighty pounds or I might be tempted to go up to a hundred, after all, it was a smasher. Entering this quaint emporium was like stepping back in time, dark mahogany furniture, two huge leather armchairs and two ageing shop assistants, a lady in a black dress and a string of pearls and a gentleman who looked for all the world like John Le Mesurier wearing a green velvet jacket and a bow tie. He welcomed me like a long-lost relative, informing me that I had arrived with perfect timing. It was their Christmas 10% discount day.

I explained that I was quite interested in the watch in the window and he invited me to take a seat in one of the huge luxurious leather armchairs, and immediately I felt like Ronnie Corbett doing one of his famous monologues on the "Two Ronnies". As he marched towards the window, he said: "Would sir care for a glass of mead? After all, it is nearly Christmas."

I said that would be very nice.

"Maureen dear, please get sir a glass of mead, and a shortbread biscuit."

He returned and slipped the watch on my wrist. There was no denying, it looked the business. So there I was, glass of mead in one hand, shortbread biscuit in the other, with all three of us admiring my potentially new time piece. "Oh, Maureen," said the Dads' Army lookalike. "Don't you think that watch was made for sir?" My glass was topped up as he made seasonal small talk, but I decided that it was time to get down to business. "How Much?" All the time I was thinking "Don't forget, a hundred quid top whack". He reached for his calculator and said, very matter of factly: "Well, Sir, taking into account the very generous 10% discount it comes to one thousand, two hundred and…" I didn't get the rest and I didn't need to. Twelve hundred quid for a watch? Who do these people think I am, Lord Nuffield. I know full well I should have bounded off my chair and said, "Sorry guys, way out of my league, but happy Christmas and thanks for the wine". But they had been so charming, even if it was professionally rehearsed charm. I was speechless, but just then he threw me a lifeline. He had noticed that the watch was a bit too big for my pathetically girlie wrist and told me that the "in-house horologist" would be back off his lunch (looking at HIS watch) in nine or ten minutes and if I had any further shopping to do he would have it fitting perfectly and polished in half an hour. "Brilliant," I gleefully exclaimed and turned to head out of the shop. "We will have to ask for a small deposit, sir, as a gesture of goodwill," said our man. I reached into my wallet for a fiver, thinking that it was a small price to pay for such a narrow escape. "We normally ask for £50 for an item of this price." I felt the blood draining from my face as I handed over my bank card. What a pillock I'd been. Of course, I never went back to the shop and just put it all down to experience.

When Lulu was booked to appear on the breakfast show to plug her new album I thought, "Great, a chance to get my own back for that dirty look." I had decided that I would defy convention and start the interview by saying, "Good God, Lulu, you've let yourself go," but come the big day I totally lost my bottle and couldn't go through with it. I did remind her of our meeting all those years ago and how much I'd been stung by that dirty look, but although she admitted to remembering me, she was adamant that she had never given me the skunk eye. Oh, yes you did, girl.

One morning, completely out of the blue, I received an e-mail from Penny Mellor, she had tracked me down via Facebook, and she suggested

I get in touch with Bill and arrange a pint or two. I was over the moon to hear from her and once again flabbergasted to realise that after all these years they were still together. So, following a couple of tentative e-mails, me and my old best mate met up on neutral ground, the Cresta Court Hotel in Altrincham. It was like nothing had happened, we chatted away for hours about holidays, the family and, of course, football. Bill has been a dedicated Manchester City season ticket holder for donkey's years and although I never expected to see City being the dominant force in Manchester, let alone football in general, I couldn't begrudge someone like Bill his long-awaited good fortune. I'm delighted to say that the meetings have become a regular occurrence and we are the best of friends once again. Lynn has met Penny and they also got on very well. Just a pity it all took so long, forty lost years.

I stayed on the Signal 2 Breakfast Show for a record-breaking 15 years. Nobody in the history of Signal Radio had survived on breakfast for so long and indeed only a handful of people have lasted anywhere near that length of time doing a breakfast show anywhere. It takes it out of you, believe me. I only decided to leave when some genius decided to change the music policy, despite the fact that Signal 2 was just about the most successful medium wave station in the country. Over the years we had featured an eclectic mix of 60s 70s and 80s songs, but now it was decreed that in the popular pursuit of a younger listenership, we should scrap all the 60s music as well as most of the 70s and go heavy on the 80s. I soon became disheartened by having to play the same songs over and over again, especially when I had never really liked them the first time round. As I mentioned the 80s invoked largely bad memories for me, so I made up my mind to come off breakfast and move to weekends, where I was promised a free hand. It was also comforting to know that I had left of my own free will, not many people in radio get to do that. As I said many times over the years, no gold watches are dished out in the world of radio.

I mentioned earlier about the importance of audience participation in my shows. In fact, listener involvement was always crucial to my radio output. I always tried to create an atmosphere in which the listener felt that they belonged to some kind of private members club. Without wishing to make it bigger than it was, I would wake up every morning determined to create great radio, a show that people would talk about in the factory or the office. I created "The Five Foot Five and a Half Inches Club" solely for listeners who were exactly that height, and I myself was the founding member and life president. Then there was the "A over T club", A over T standing for arse over tit. To be eligible, you had to have come a cropper in the icy conditions of mid-winter.

On top of this, we did "Have you ever met a murderer?" and "Does your first name rhyme with your surname?". My favourite caller on this topic was a lady called Sue, who was married to a half-Chinese dentist called Michael Hoo, so she was Sue Hoo and he was Dr Hoo. Brilliant!

Then there was "Has a famous person ever said to you: Do you know who I am?" The very first caller on that subject was a lady who said that, while working in a department store, she served a very posh woman who was demanding a big discount, declaring, "My dear woman, you must know who I am!" It was the one and only Fanny Craddock. Which brings me to my favourite Fanny Craddock story, which might well be apocryphal but, nevertheless, made it onto my show.

It concerns Fanny's famous television cookery show co-hosted in the 60s by her comfortably imbibed husband Johnny. On this particular programme, Fanny was telling us how to make doughnuts, and at the end of the show Johnny stepped forward to say, "Here's hoping your doughnuts turn out just like Fanny's."

I started to get phone calls from a chap in Wigan called Jimmy who, despite being wheelchair bound, was a happy, cheerful soul with a great sense of humour. His distinctive voice, very much like the actor Joe Gladwin who played Nora Batty's long-suffering husband in "Last of the Summer Wine", made me think that the listeners would really warm to him, so I started to include him in the show. And I was right. Jimmy soon became a star of the show, and I gave him his own feature entitled "Jimmy's Riddle" in which he would give out a cryptic clue as to the identity of a pop star. For example: "You can have him for lunch or have him for tea, but never for breakfast, it's two out of three." The answer, of course, was Meatloaf.

Another popular feature was "The film in five seconds game" where I would act out the title of a well-known film. For example: "Well we have had a wonderful morning, we've seen the lions, the tigers and the elephants, but right now I need the toilet". I won't insult your intelligence by giving you the answer. None of these things taken individually were ever likely to change the world, let alone the face of radio, but together they helped to shape an interesting and thought-provoking breakfast show.

With working on Christmas morning every year for so long, it had become something of a tradition to open our presents on Christmas Eve, so on the 24th of December 2018 despite having the following day off, we continued the tradition. We had our Christmas Eve buffet of pork pies, pate, cheese and crackers and got stuck into both the presents and the wine. Our next-door neighbours Dave and Carol knocked on with a couple of glasses of sherry and it was a lovely relaxed evening. My gorgeous grandson

Sean had been born a month earlier and we were excitedly making plans to go over to Australia to see the little chap. I woke up on Christmas morning feeling refreshed and positive about the year ahead, and I paid hardly any attention to what I thought was a bout of indigestion. Just a bit too much wine and food the night before.

Little did I realise that it was the start of the worst and most terrifying year of my life.

After goodness knows how many injections and scans I was eventually rushed into hospital with severe jaundice. "I'm afraid you have cancer of the bile duct" said Mr Chilie, my consultant, "It's very rare and quite aggressive " I didn't even know I had a bile duct, what is it ? What does it do ? . The "C" word is a word that nobody wants to be confronted with and I am no different. I did get emotional and embarrassingly the first question I asked was "How long have I got ? Immediately I regretted asking such a stupid question, surely everybody asks that. The jaundice meant that it was too dangerous to begin treatment immediately so I had to wait what seemed like an eternity before anything could be done. I have been on a tour of hospitals this year and been given months rather than years. I am having chemotherapy every week at the moment and at the time of writing I feel no pain and people keep telling me how well I look. My answer is always the same " You should see me from the inside". Lynn has been wonderfully supportive throughout and she even encouraged me to get back on the radio which I have done . A Sunday afternoon show on the brilliant Hitmix Radio has given me a new lease of life. How long for ???? time will tell.

CHAPTER 16: "There Must Be an Angel", The Eurythmics 1985 (Number 1)

A friend of mine once said that he thought I must have a guardian angel sitting on my shoulder watching out for me, because whatever scrape I got myself into, I usually got out of it fairly unscathed. So … where are you now guardian angel?

On reflection I think my mate had a point. Certainly, up until now, I have led pretty much a charmed life. Despite leaving 'Grange Street Secondary Modern School' without so much as a 25 metre swimming certificate, (although in my day it would have been yards), and being a major disappointment to my Mum in terms of never 'getting a proper job with a decent pension', I think I have escaped the trials and tribulations of everyday life and done alright. I have pretty much beaten the system! I spent most of my working life doing a job I loved, even though on the face of it, I had no right whatsoever to infiltrate the heady world of broadcasting. I certainly never studied media or received any training whatsoever. Sorry, but I spent 40 years busking it, and even today on the brilliant Hitmix Radio I am still making it up as I go along.

Who would have thought, for example, that thirty years after being mistaken for David Essex on a petrol station forecourt in Rochdale, I would find myself interviewing the great man and asking him if he could see a resemblance? Sadly, he couldn't. Meeting the great Gerry Anderson many years ago remains a highlight. A lovely bloke who, when I asked him an obscure question about his early children's television series "Four Feather Falls" (ask your Grandad, kids) he didn't know the answer. However, as soon as he got home and having done a bit of research, he faxed me the all the information I asked for and plenty more. I'm sorry but I can't for the life of me remember the question.

Being invited to air my views on the Presidential election campaign live on an American radio station was also a memorable occasion, but again, please don't ask me what I said because knowing absolutely bugger all about American politics I was once again just busking it …. no change there then!

Had I not met 'Mad' Malc Dixon at Burton the Tailor's all those years ago, I may have spent most of my life taking down inside leg measurements!

Many years ago, live on air, I had my handwriting studied by a graphologist who didn't know it was my handwriting. This is what he concluded ….

"Now this handwriting is so spontaneous, so original, that it is almost jumping out from the page. This writer wants attention, and he's determined to get it.
He is intelligent, ambitious and he's got a vivid imagination (imagination + concentration + ability = signs that could lead to writing or authorship). He can be extremely talkative and sociable, but he can also be a loner at times.
HE CAN HAVE MOOD SWINGS FROM BEING CHARMING TO IRRITABLE.

He expects accuracy from others, yet due to his haste is often careless himself. Interfere with his plans and expect a strong reaction. He is independent and likes to do things his own way. His writing shows emotion, strongly suggesting a link to the past. Childhood experiences definitely hold a certain dominance over his life. He is fiercely protective of those near and dear to him. Life has certainly had its drawbacks for this writer but his determination has paid dividends and will continue to do so, as he reaches his ultimate goal"

Everybody I ever show this to says the same thing, "that's you in a nutshell, mate"

It's amazing how your ultimate goal alters as your circumstances change. I was watching England on telly the other night and the commentator announced that they had now qualified for the European Championships next June. My immediate thought was "I only hope I'm still here". By the way God … if you are reading this … I would very much like to come back as a Premier League footballer next time … if that's alright with you. Although knowing my luck I'll probably return as a camel, schlepping up and down the Gobi Desert all day and night spitting at the tourists. I know, that's a bit rich, talking about how lucky I have been and then dismissing it. Maybe coming back as a beast of burden would serve me right!

When it comes to presenting radio shows, I'm the first to admit that I'm a bit of a one trick pony. I only have the one show in me, plenty of trivia, lots of listener interaction and as little 'dee-jay speak' as I can get away with. I also hate being taken out of my comfort zone. Maybe that stems from the aforementioned lack of formal training. Of course, things have changed a lot since the advent of the 'World Wide Web'. Years ago, I could set a trivia question and it might run for weeks at a time and listeners would be determined to be the first to come up with the answer. Sadly, these days they just google it. I still do love to dig out really obscure bits of trivia and every show that I do, I like to give the listener at least a couple of things to talk about over a cup of coffee at work.

Here are a few of my favourites from over the years...

Irene Ryan, who played Granny Clampett in the Beverley Hillbillies was the first white woman to record an album on the Tamla Motown Record Label.

Most people are aware that Debbie Harry was adopted, but not too many people are aware that her birth name was Angela Tremble.

When Carry on Star Kenneth Williams made his television debut his father was so embarrassed by his performance that he committed suicide on the very same day. Kenneth was questioned by Scotland Yard on suspicion of killing his dad,

'Telstar' man Joe Meek was the number one suspect in the 'Body in the bag' murder case when he shot his landlady before turning the gun on himself.

Nelson Mandela's real name was Roly Lala.

Barry Manilow turned down the part of 'Ted the pilot' in the comedy smash 'Airplane'.

Elvis Presley, Judy Garland and King George III all died on the toilet.

Right ... back to the story.

CHAPTER 17: "When You Walk in the Room", The Searchers 1964 (Number 3)

My initial idea was to end the book at Chapter 15 because I didn't think people would want to hear about the gruesome year I have just had. And, I really didn't feel like writing about it. However, everybody from my wife, to friends, to colleagues and yes even the publishers were adamant - the full story should be told. Of course, when I say the full story, I mean the full story so far.

So ... I'd woken up on Christmas morning with what I thought was indigestion. By the middle of January, the problem was still there and it had been joined by spasmodic stomach pains, so I thought it was time to make an appointment at the doctors. To be honest, Lynn's mum Margaret had been the first person to notice something was not quite right before Christmas. She mentioned that I looked 'a bit yellow' and under the weather. However, I could not for the life of me see what she was getting at so I ignored her, I certainly couldn't see any signs of jaundice and at that time I felt absolutely fine. The doctor carried out a blood test and the results were a bit scary - liver swollen and cholesterol through the roof! Lynn said when I got back home, I looked like I'd seen a ghost. "That's it" I said, "today is the first day of the rest of my life - no more booze and healthy eating from now on". To be honest the timing could have been a bit better - Lynn had just got back from Tesco with four bottles of red wine, two bottles of white, a bottle of Gin and a couple of Pizzas! By the way, when did they invent cholesterol? No such thing in my day!

It's now two weeks since I last had a drink. People tell me that they have never felt better since giving up the booze but, to be honest, I have never felt worse. How come everything you enjoy is deemed bad for you? Why can't wine, fish chips and mushy peas be an essential part of your five a day?

At the beginning of February, the stomach pains had not gone away, so the doctor booked me in for a gastroscopy, that's a wire that goes down your throat with a camera on the end. At the time it was the most horrendous thing I have ever had to endure, for one thing I expected the 'wire' to be about as thick as a piece of cotton but this thing was more like something you find in a car wash. It took half a dozen exasperated nurses three or four attempts to successfully conduct the procedure because I was squirming and squealing like a big girl's blouse. However, it was all clear - nothing untoward going on down there.

The stomach pains were now getting worse and Lynn's mum had noticed an increase in the jaundice, but to be honest I still couldn't see it. I was having big problems sleeping and would spend most of the night on the settee watching old movies on the talking pictures channel. One day when Lynn had gone out shopping, I decided to take myself off to bed because I couldn't keep my eyes open. As I was drifting off to sleep, I thought I'd better put my boxer shorts back on because I didn't want anybody finding me dead in bed naked. That's how paranoid I'd become.

On the 12th of February 2019, I was extremely sad to hear the news that the great Gordon Banks had passed away. Over the years I had the immense pleasure of meeting Gordon on numerous occasions and he was just a lovely man, and of course, the number one goalie of all time. I was leaving the house that very day and bumped into my neighbour, 'Dave the Gasman'.

The conversation went like this …

Me: … shame about Banksy isn't it Dave?
Dave: … how d'yer mean?
Me: … he's passed away … it's all over the news.
Dave: … blimey … how old was he?
Me: … eighty one
Dave: … never!! I didn't think he was that old!
Me: … well they are all getting on a bit now
Dave: … how d'yer mean?
Me: … The World Cup lads …. all getting on a bit
Dave: … oh … that Banksy … I thought you meant the bloke who paints on walls!

By the way, Dave is a Liverpool fan …. enough said! I can't help thinking that Gordon would have found that conversation hilarious.

I have been booked into Leighton Hospital in Crewe for an abdominal scan. Hopefully, they can at last track down what is causing these increasingly painful stomach pains and cramps that have been dogging me for a couple of months. Apparently, the scan showed up a slight blockage in my bile duct, whatever that is, so now it's back to hospital for more tests.

11th March 2019. I have been trying to make an appointment with the doctor for weeks now but she is always booked up. Lynn has now noticed the yellowness and says I look like a creature from a 1950's science fiction B movie, and I have to say I feel really poorly. Eventually, I'm granted an evening telephone consultation - I just hope she hasn't got anything planned for the evening because I've got a lot to say.

The jaundice is now evident to everyone, even me. My urine is the colour of treacle and what is coming out of the other end could be damp clay which refuses to flush, and I feel completely shattered all the time. I can sense that the doctor is becoming ever more concerned and she says she is going to try and get me into hospital that very night. She will phone me back in ten minutes. When she does phone back, she tells me that having taken advice there is no need for me to go into hospital straight away but she will make an urgent appointment for me to see a specialist. Four weeks later I get a letter telling me an appointment has been made ... in three weeks' time. So that's the medical profession's definition of urgent is it?

I didn't get to see the specialist at the appointment, probably too busy, but I did get to see his cheerful, happy, smiling Chinese registrar. Following a bit of poking about he said "You are quite yellow". I replied "My wife thinks I look like a Chinaman", then realising that he was himself Chinese I added "No Offence" which probably didn't help! Anyway, the upshot was more tests.

22nd April. I had to get Lynn to telephone Signal and tell them that I didn't think I'd ever be well enough to return to the show. When I gave up the Breakfast Show in order to move to the weekend we had plans to do so much, but you just never know what's around the corner. Soon afterwards I got a call from the hospital telling me I needed to be admitted right away. No delays get here now! To be honest I was quite relieved - something was finally happening.

Now the first thing I want to say is that the doctors, nurses and assistants do a magnificent job under extreme pressure! Even the food is pretty much beyond reproach considering the number of mouths they have to feed! But, everybody I spoke to, staff included, agreed that night time in hospital is horrendous! Let me tell you about Ward 13 at Leighton Hospital in Crewe 'after dark'. Firstly, there was William, a very well educated, well-spoken church warden, a lovely man with impeccable manners but his snoring defied description! Completely off the Richter Scale! Then there was old Joe, well, I called him 'old Joe' until I discovered he was three years older than me! Joe suffered from earth shattering wind which didn't seem to wake him up but certainly woke the rest of the hospital.

An honourable mention for really old Jack, 86 years old and dreadfully confused. Constantly shouting "what time is it" to nobody in particular and every 20 minutes or so he would let out a blood curdling scream. One night the nurse rushed in which in itself was a novelty and said "Are you alright Jack"? "Yes" said the old fellow "I'm just relieving the boredom". Thanks for that Jack, mate. We also had a regular interloper who I christened 'Wandering Walter' who would shuffle in about three times a night shouting "has anyone seen my wife" closely followed by three or four exasperated nurses who would breathlessly drag him out again. Oh, and not forgetting the chap who would come in to say 'hello' at three o'clock in the morning completely oblivious to what time it was, and also the fact that he was stark bollock naked!

Then there was the hospital equipment. The innocent looking machine that is used to attach you to a drip. It was supposed to bleep when it had finished its cycle or developed a fault, but in truth, it started bleeping the moment the nurse left the ward and continued bleeping for most of the night. As the patients cursed, the professionals seemed oblivious to the racket - phones constantly ringing, buzzers buzzing and various things alarming. I christened Ward 13 "The Ghost Train" because every thirty seconds or so something would startle you or make you jump out of your skin.

One day, the little cheerful Chinese registrar turned up and asked me if we could go somewhere quiet to talk. I followed him to this little room that up until now I didn't know existed. It seemed very neglected with dilapidated faded furniture, threadbare carpets, a small television propped up on a 'seen better days' coffee table. He was about to say something when I was woken up by Lynn. I had drifted off to sleep and it was visiting time. I'd been dreaming.

The following day Mr Chilie the specialist finally put in an appearance. Once again it was visiting time and once again Lynn was on hand. Mr Chilie was accompanied by a lady who I assumed was his assistant but eagle-eyed Lynn had spotted her lapel badge. She was a Senior McMillan Nurse. This time it was Mr Chilie's turn to ask if we could go somewhere private to talk, but this was no dream.

As soon as we entered the room a million shivers went down my spine. The neglected dilapidated faded furniture. Threadbare carpets and the small television propped up on the 'seen better days' coffee table. It was here. It was real. I sensed immediately what was coming.

"I'm afraid you have cancer of the bile duct" said Mr Chilie looking at his shoes rather than at me. It wouldn't be the last time a specialist would concentrate on his shoes rather than look me in the eye. "It's quite a rare form of cancer and very aggressive" he continued, before asking if Lynn and I would like some time alone. For the first and only time I had a little cry and so did Lynn.

The usual emotions overcame me. Why me? What had I done to deserve this? You hear stories all the time of good for nothing parasites conning vulnerable dementia suffering old folk out of their life savings by promising to do some work on the house or whatever, then disappearing. Why can't they be struck down? I have never knowingly hurt anybody in my life.

THIS IS JUST NOT FAIR.

CHAPTER 18: "Shakin' All Over", Johnny Kidd 1960 (Number One)

24th April 2019. Got the shock of my life yesterday. I looked in the bathroom mirror and my dear old mum was staring back at me. I went downstairs and said to Lynn "I've aged ten years in two weeks". My beloved didn't attempt any soft soap "Yes I know" she agreed, "I was just thinking the same thing myself". The truth is I need an operation and I need It yesterday, but it can't be done while I'm still jaundiced, apparently the risk of infection is too great. The doctors settled on a "procedure" an interim investigation under local anaesthetic using keyhole surgery. Apparently, this "procedure" is beyond Leighton Hospital so it was decided that I should be transferred to The Royal Stoke University Hospital. With the help of Lynn and her mother off I went. The Royal Stoke is a place that the people of Stoke-on-Trent should be proud of. A very impressive building more like an airport than a hospital. Absolutely massive. I got there about one in the afternoon and was put in an assessment ward and was told that the doctor would examine me as soon as he could. At about 4 o'clock I was asked If I wanted to something to eat. By this time, I could have eaten a horse between two bread bins so I snapped their hands off. "Well" said the nurse we have fish, chips and mushy peas or …", "I'll have that" I gleefully interrupted. Half an hour later the fish supper appeared complete with a sachet of salt and a sachet of vinegar and very appetising it looked. I was just tearing open the sachet of vinegar and licking my lips when the young nurse re-appeared and snatched the tray way. "Sorry" she said "nil by mouth till you have seen the doctor". It was like a dagger through my hungry heart. "You can't put fish and chips in front of a starving man then snatch it away... that's cruel beyond belief". The young nurse's bottom lip started to quiver before mumbling something about "orders is orders" and disappearing with the fish supper. By 8 o'clock nothing had happened and Lynn and her mum were visibly wilting so I ordered them to bugger off home assuring them that I would be OK.

I waited and waited for this mysterious doctor to arrive. At about 9.30 a junior doctor turned up, asked me a few questions and assured me that the senior doctor would be along presently. Just before eleven he finally appeared; he was about the same age as the junior doctor! 'It's not just coppers who are getting younger' asked the same questions as his junior counterpart and left but not before telling me that I could now finally have something to eat. "Would you like your fish, chips and mushy peas now?" said the nurse. I genuinely couldn't think of anything I would like more, although I never imagined that it would be the same fish, chips and mushy peas, complete with half opened vinegar sachet that had been served up earlier. By now it was cold, congealed and completely inedible. That night I had a tube of smarties out of the vending machine for my supper.

The following day I went for an MRI scan. A new experience and one I never want to repeat. I was told it would be noisy, and it was. An incredible din. I was told there would be music to distract from the noise and I would receive clear instructions. I was placed inside this Flash Gordon style space rocket type thingy (there's one for the teenagers) and off I went. What a horrible half an hour that was! It felt as if an army of people were hammering on the roof! There were lights and laser's flashing on and off. The only thing I couldn't hear was any music. And the so called 'instructions' sounded like they were being delivered by Bill and Ben dubbed in German. I'm afraid I had a bit of a panic attack. All I could hear was one of the nurses shouting "please keep still". Easy for her to say. The following day would be down to the theatre for the procedure. I really couldn't wait. Something was to be done at last. The nurses in theatre were lovely, as was the lady surgeon who explained everything that was about to happen. A bit too much information to be honest but hey ho! Then a foppish young chap introduced himself as somebody who would be 'assisting the surgeon'. Then he turned to one of the nurses and asked where the kitchen was. "Right over there" she said "the door marked Kitchen" … "Oh" replied the foppish fellow "I've never noticed that before"! I thought to myself, here's a bloke who can't find his way to the kitchen even though it's clearly marked 'kitchen', yet he's expecting to find his way round my body using keyhole surgery. When I came round, I was told that the procedure had been reasonably successful, only later did I discover that it had been anything but. I was supposed to be having what they call a stent fitted which would do the job of the failed bile duct, but by now the tumour was too big and the surgeon had given up trying. Instead I had been fitted with two drain bags coming out of either side of my body with pipes running down my legs connected to plastic bags to collect the waste bile. This was a whole new low. I hated these drain bags, hated them, hated them. Hated them. I felt dirty, old and decrepit.

A couple of days later I was told I could go home and although I definitely didn't feel well enough to go anywhere, if the experts said I could go, then I was off. I got home staggered up to bed and stayed there 'til the next morning. Saturday and Sunday morning passed without incident but without any warning at all I was suddenly hit by an agonising stomach pain. Like nothing I had ever experienced before. It felt like I was being repeatedly stabbed. I also became freezing cold, shaking, shivering and my teeth were actually chattering like a character from a Tom and Jerry cartoon. I staggered upstairs put a jumper on, put on my big woolly fleece, told Lynn to put the heating on and crawled into bed. While Lynn made the call to Leighton Hospital, I lay there in agony shaking and shivering and thinking about my Dad who had a heart attack on a Sunday, forty odd years ago. Being a Sunday, it took forever for the ambulance to arrive and by the time it did, it was too late. Over the years I always thought to myself "whatever you do ...don't get ill on a Sunday". And here I was. However, an hour or so later two lovely female paramedics arrived. "Oh my God" said one of the girls "you look like a hot banana" referring I think to my jaundice. Well that immediately set me off thinking about the Elvis song that begins with the line " hot banana, hot, hot banana, hot banana ..yeh" was it Teddy Bear or King Creole? Before I could make my mind up the paramedic said "Take your fleece off, take your jumper off, turn the heating off and open the windows". "What are you talking about" I replied, "I'm freezing cold, I feel like I'm naked on top of Mount Everest". I was told that I only thought I was cold and in fact my temperature was off the scale. I was in fact boiling hot! To cut a long story shortish after a 5 hour wait in A&E I was back on ward 13 in Leighton, this time in a room all to myself. Just me, four walls, and that dreaded bleeping machine which, of course, right on cue, started bleeping the moment the nurse left the room. When she eventually came back, I said "Do you know nurse if it wasn't for that machine I might just book for the same week next year. She chuckled and said "Glad to see you've still got your sense of humour". I was trying to keep my pecker up. If you have ever been in hospital you will have noticed that somehow the nurses know the moment you have finally managed to nod off, that's when they come rushing in and wake you up to take your blood pressure. I was so drugged up that I began hallucinating and having really bad nightmares involving being chased and bitten by dogs. I genuinely thought this was it. I was about to die, and to be honest I didn't care. I am not brave and have never pretended to be, I was in real pain and I didn't like it one bit.

26th April 2019. Mr Chilie paid a visit to the ward today. I think It's fair to say that Lynn has fallen head over heels for Mr Chilie and even I can understand why. Tall and tanned and very good looking, a mouthful of pearly whites and always immaculately dressed, he is a fine figure of a man, which makes me all the more aware of my current pathetic state. Especially these disgusting drain bags, and the fact that I am losing weight at such a rate that pretty soon there will surely be nothing left of me. Mr Chilie wants to refer me to yet another hospital. The Queen Elizabeth in Birmingham. He explains that they have a brilliant reputation and they are famous for not giving up on people. When every other hospital in the

Country admits defeat, these guys will keep trying. Sounds just what I need. Co-incidentally, we were watching a programme about the hospital just a few days earlier; Surgeons removed the equivalent of an 8 stone human being from a woman's body during an eight-hour operation. When they deposited the mound of fat on the slab it looked for all the world like a beached whale. Then they operated on a poor bloke who was bent double with severe back problems. After the twelve-hour op it reminded me of the 'Only Fools' episode where Del Boy is trying to flog this bogus back cure on the market. At a pre-arranged time Uncle Albert staggers past on crutches. One application from Del and he turns into Gene Kelly in Singing in the Rain!

A couple of weeks later I found myself travelling to Birmingham to see yet another consultant who shook me firmly by the hand and said "Call Me Nick". He explained that they needed to do some up to date tests to see how far the cancer has spread and I'll be left with three options:

1. Do nothing and I'll be dead by Christmas
2. Chemotherapy which will give me about 12 months
3. An operation to remove most of my liver which will entail 2 weeks in intensive care but might give me 5 years.

No prizes for guessing which option I went for. What an absolute nightmare this year is turning out to be.

According to the district nurse, when I was rushed into hospital with an infection a couple of weeks earlier, I had sepsis and the staff at Leighton were really concerned that I wouldn't pull through. Probably just as well nobody mentioned it at the time or I might have had a heart attack. A bit in limbo at the moment waiting to hear from Birmingham. The nurse also said that her father in law had exactly the same illness as me and the people at The Queen Elizabeth Hospital saved his life when everybody else had given up on him although he had to have lots of operations.

2nd May 2019. Still not heard from the hospital and to be honest, I'm starting to crumble a bit. If I don't hear anything in the morning, I might try the "do you know who I am" ploy, that should give them a bit of a laugh. Went for a paper this morning and the girl said "Oh I haven't seen you for …. oh my God, you look terrible"! I explained that I had not been well and she said "Not well ...you look like you've been dug up". She must have missed the 'be tactful' training day! I did mention that this illness has made me age 10 years in a few weeks but I wasn't expecting everybody else to notice.

Years ago, when I still lived in Manchester, I used to go to a lovely lady dentist every few months for a check-up and she would always greet me with the words, "everything OK?". I'm sure she meant with my teeth but

I always replied, "well I'm skint and am no longer attractive to women but I don't suppose you can help with that". No matter how many times she heard it she always had the good grace to chuckle. I thought about that in the paper shop this morning.

8th May 2019. Decided to go to the doctors this morning and she took yet another blood test. I know it's a cliché but my arms really are like an old dartboard at the moment. 'Just a little scratch' seems to have replaced 'Just a little prick' as the pre- jab warning these days. The doc did say that I might well end up back in hospital if the tests came back a bit dodgy. She has prescribed liquid morphine so with a bit of luck I might get a decent night's kip tonight.... although liquid morphine does sound a bit grown up.

13th May 2019. Finally had a call from the Queen Elizabeth Hospital this morning but I'm afraid it was not great news. Apparently, the cancer has spread from my bile duct to my liver and I will need 80% of my liver removed before I can have the operation to tackle the cancer. I have to go back to Birmingham a week tomorrow, not for the procedure but to sign a consent form. Then I'll go back on the waiting list. By all accounts it takes five or six weeks for the liver to re-grow itself. So, that's another six weeks after I have had the procedure. In the meantime, here I am, dying of cancer. Yes, you're right. I am feeling very sorry for myself. Feeling a bit abandoned at the moment. My consultant tells me that I have a very aggressive form of the disease but nobody seems to be in any kind of rush to do anything about it. I did offer to sign the consent forms when I saw the consultant nearly three weeks ago but was told this was not a priority. The thing is, apart from the occasional stomach pains and feeling a bit tired all the time, I don't really feel ill at all. People keep telling me that I look quite well, my standard reply is "You should see me from the inside".

24th May 2019. Just back from a long and tiring day at The Queen Elizabeth Hospital but after having a long discussion with the consultant I feel a bit more confident that I can beat this horrible disease than I did before. He showed me a photo of the scan that I had on Sunday and explained that the tumour was no worse than when I had the last one more than two months ago. That was a huge relief because that had been bothering me. Then he told me what was to happen next. Because the cancer in my bile duct had spread to my liver they would have to get rid of over half the liver and wait for it to re-grow itself. The reason all this has taken so long is because when I was first diagnosed, I was badly jaundiced and they couldn't do anything because of the risk of infection. Then I got the sepsis thing and now they have to get rid of the old liver and wait for the new one. The consultant was very nice and patiently went through what needed to happen step by step. I was told the only problem would be if the liver refused to play ball. Basically, if that happens it's 'Goodnight Vienna', but he seemed pretty relaxed about it. "Is there anything I can or can't do to help the process"? I asked. He said apart from not smoking or drinking I just had to relax and hope for the best. Well, as I must be one of the few people in Britain, at least of a certain age that has never had a cigarette in his life that was no problem. To this day I can't even bear to touch a cigarette. As regards the drink I said to the doctor "I certainly won't be doing that, it's what got me in this mess in the first place". Then he said that the type of cancer I had was nothing to do with alcohol and that I was just unlucky. That was a relief because I didn't want it getting around that I'd drunk myself to death! And Lynn would have to stop calling me "self-inflicted Sid" after the character in Minder played by the great Ronnie Frazer. So it's the liver thing in a week or so then the big cancer op in four or five weeks depending how soon the liver gets a move on.

7th June 2019. Travel to hospital on Sunday then the liver procedure on Monday followed by a couple of days recovery in hospital. The doctors In Birmingham assure me that they do this kind of operation all the time. I dare say that's the case but as far as I'm concerned relieving somebody of 80% of his liver is a big deal! Lynn and I were chatting last night and she said that the ideal scenario was that both operations go well and by Christmas I could be fit enough to think about going to Australia for a couple of months.

I agreed that it was probably the best I could hope for, but my ideal scenario would be this ……...

I wake up on Monday and the surgeon is standing over me smiling broadly. He is holding something between his thumb and his index finger. … "We were all sure it was a tumour weren't we lads" he says looking round at his colleagues, "but no … it was this … a salted peanut lodged in your bile duct " A salted bloody peanut ..that's all it was. "Mr Owen" he continues "you can go home, open a bottle of champagne and take this salted peanut with you to keep as a souvenir". At which point everybody in the operating theatre bursts into a spontaneous round of applause followed by a rousing chorus of "for he's a jolly good fellow".

That's my ideal scenario!

13th June 2019. Well, I'm bruised, battered and beaten but still here. I feel like I have been punched in the stomach for ten rounds by Tyson Fury. If the last few days are an indication of what's to come then it's a bit scary. I could not believe how many people were in the theatre helping with my procedure. The roll call must have taken 20 minutes before they put me to sleep. And I wonder why they bother to check your blood pressure just before putting you to sleep! Surely, it's bound to be sky high? Having finished my tour of NHS Hospitals, I think I'm in a decent position to report back. The Surgeons and Consultants at the QE are rightly rated as the best in the world but the nursing staff in Birmingham are hit and miss. Depending on who's on duty they either can't do enough for you or can barely do enough. And the food was diabolical. I've been living on ice cream since Monday and not proper ice cream, I'm talking about those little tubs you used to get in the pictures with the wooden spoon. Much like Leighton Hospital, the QE turned into a madhouse at night. One nurse in particular had no decibel control whatsoever, whether she was on duty at two in the afternoon or two in the morning everything was conducted at full volume. After turning all the lights on of course. If you're going into hospital expecting to rest and relax, forget it!

A big hello to my new FB friend 'Rob the Brummie' who made life bearable during my stay. Despite the fact that he thinks Corbyn would make a great PM (I was too sore to argue) he was a very decent bloke and the only person on the ward who wasn't either semi-conscious, gaga or both. Take dear old Sidney for instance, 98 years old, as deaf as a post and not a clue what was going on. He spent most of the night screaming at the top of his voice for a bed-pan, when the nurse eventually turned up, the question was always "What do you want Sidney?" I'm thinking all he ever wants is a bed pan! Why not just bring a bed pan in the first place and save time! The nurse then usually said that they would be back soon with a bed pan. Half an hour later when they did return Sidney would announce at the top of his voice that they were too late, he had done it in the bed. The thing is that for about two minutes every day Sid was pretty lucid and he seemed a genuinely nice, polite bloke and this was certainly no way to end your days.

One thing I've learned is that if a member of the nursing staff says they will be back in two minutes, give it two hours. If they haven't returned after that, the chances are you'll never see them again. I'm booked in for a scan in three weeks to make sure everything is going to plan and I have been instructed to eat lots of chicken and fish. I can manage that.

15th June 2019. Think I spoke too soon. I was rushed back into hospital yesterday with severe stomach pains but back the following day thankfully, with Marc, Jacquie and Sean who have taken time off from a wedding in Spain. When Marc walked in holding a happy smiling Sean, I burst into tears. I'd begun to think I wouldn't be around long enough to ever see the little chap. Marc handed Sean over and he promptly kicked me in the stomach. A right foot volley that Cristiano Ronaldo would have been proud of. With a forced smile I immediately handed him back. By the way if you've been wondering whatever happened to 'Nurse Ratched' from 'One

Flew Over the Cuckoo's Nest' fame, I am sad to report that she is alive and well and working the night shift at Leighton Hospital. Had a run in with her at 2 o'clock this morning when I woke up in a pool of my own Bile. Now there's a sentence I never thought I'd write … "woke up in a pool of my own bile".

She admitted to me that she had no idea what she was doing when she was trying to fit me with a new drain bag. I'm afraid I lost my temper and screamed at her to "stop manhandling me". I did apologise although I thought I was in the right and she should be the one saying sorry. I said that I had gone through enough just lately and I would prefer somebody who knew what they were doing. She stormed off and I heard her say to a colleague "He says he's had enough … haven't we all". That set the tone for the rest of the night. The doctors wanted me to stay in but I begged them to let me come home so I could at last meet baby Sean. I must say I became very emotional and I think they took pity on me.

23rd June 2019. I had a call from The Queen Elizabeth Hospital in Birmingham cancelling my scan for tomorrow. Apparently, they have just realised it's far too soon after my procedure to learn anything from it. I think I could have told them that. It's been put back a couple of weeks. After being assured that I was in the best possible hands and seeing the television programme about the great work that they do I'm fast losing confidence in the QE. To be honest, despite the fact that we had already bought the train tickets, I'm not too disappointed. I'm still feeling very sore and the prospect of trekking to Birmingham was a daunting one.

All in all, this is turning into the worst year of my life. I first felt a bit poorly on Christmas Day and it's been bad news ever since. What did the Queen call it? Annus Horribilis! I call it 'a bloody s***e year'.

28th June 2019. Went to see my GP Dr Hughes today for a review of what's been happening. She was concerned by the fact that I'd lost so much weight and she has put me on a high calorie diet which means I can eat apple pie and cream, pizza, toasted tea cakes, pork pies, cream cakes, curries etc without feeling guilty. Lynn is dead jealous! The district nurse has just been and felt the need to give me a hug because I'm looking so well. Either that or she was getting me mixed up with a young David Essex. Had a pain free night last night and a decent night's kip for once, thanks to the old codeine tablets.

7th July 2019. Finally, I had the long-awaited letter from The Queen Elizabeth hospital in Birmingham today. I go in for the big operation three weeks on Tuesday. It seems to have taken forever to get this far but at last there now seems to be a bit of light. I have deliberately tried not to ask too many questions just in case the answers put the wind up me, but it seems that they are going to take half my stomach away. Tony Hancock famously complained that he would be walking about with an empty arm after giving blood - he was lucky. I'll be walking about with an empty stomach. God willing. Having been on a tour of hospitals recently – Crewe, Stoke and Birmingham what worries me almost the most is that the quality of the food served in Brum was by far the worst of the lot. The memory of that congealed cottage pie is something I will take to my grave! Although, hopefully not for a while! Had a terribly painful night on Tuesday and didn't sleep a wink. As a result, I spent the whole of yesterday dead to the world. Feel a lot better today.

9th July 2019. Off to Birmingham in the morning for another CT scan. Then again on Friday for the results and a meeting with the Consultant. If he's happy with everything then it's all go for the big op in two weeks. Although the prospect frightens the life out of me it will be a relief to finally get it done. So, fingers crossed.

11th July 2019. After a painful, sleepless night last night I found myself spending most of today in Leighton Hospital. On first name terms with most of the staff there these days. Thankfully they decided not to keep me in, so it's back to The Queen Elizabeth Hospital in Birmingham tomorrow to get the results of my scan and to see if the consultants think enough progress has been made to have my big operation in just over a weeks' time. I am trying to stay positive but for every step I take forward I seem to take two back.

The one good thing about setting off for Birmingham early doors is that we get to stop off at McDonalds for a sausage and egg 'McMuffin'. Whoever invented the old sausage and egg taste sensation is a true genius. We have been travelling by car and Lynn's son Christopher has very kindly done all the driving as the journey is very long and for me, stressful. While he and Lynn chatter away I am happy to sit in the back with my own thoughts. It seems each time we go a different way to avoid traffic jams and accidents but he always seems to have the knack of finding a McDonalds in time for the all important breakfast stop.

16th July 2019. Lynn had made plans for a girl's night out tonight and was really looking forward to it but sadly it's been cancelled because her mate's father is in hospital. Lynn really deserves a night out because I haven't been very good company lately and it's not been fair on her. She certainly didn't bank on having to put up with all this when she got lumbered with me. Sometimes I feel like disappearing and going off to live in a cave while waiting for the inevitable but I haven't got the energy.

26th July 2019. Off to Birmingham again to make preparations for the life-saving operation. I saw the nurse who weighed me, filled in the required forms and declared me fit to be operated on. Next it was the anaesthetist who explained the procedure and the pitfalls and asked me if I was happy to proceed. I was. I was just on my way out of the hospital when another nurse caught up with me and said Dr Nick wanted a word. As soon as I got in his office, I smelled a rat. For one thing he couldn't bring himself to look at me, he was looking at his shoes. I'd seen that look before. The cancer had spread to the good part of my liver therefore an operation was impossible and now I had just the two options - do nothing and curl up and die or undergo chemotherapy which "might" give me a few months. "Whatever we tell you will be wrong" said Nick helpfully.

Whenever I find myself thinking that things can't possibly get any worse. They do.

Dr Nick did say that at least they could have a go at putting the stents in even though it had proved beyond the good people at the Royal Stoke. He said that at least this would mean that the vile drain bags could at last be removed. Well, I was definitely up for that. Another operation to look forward to.

5th August 2019. While I was waiting to hear from Birmingham I was summoned back to Leighton for a meeting with the Oncologist, Dr Jamil, about my upcoming chemotherapy. He went through the long list of possible side effects but the good thing was that apparently with the type of chemo I was due to have at least my hair would not be falling out. Some good news at last. Dr Jamil did kind of blot his copy book by saying that all they could offer me was a few months, he was looking at his shoes when he said it. All this was of course dependant on whether or not Birmingham could successfully insert these pesky stents

14th August 2019. On being wheeled to the operating theatre at the Queen Elizabeth hospital I admit it, I was petrified! I'd been told that I would be awake all the way through the procedure but to be honest, I'd rather have been knocked out. I had been suffering from really acute stomach pains for a few weeks and now they were planning to poke around in my tummy for at least an hour. As I lay on the operating table in absolute agonising pain I thought, not for the first time, that if the Good Lord called me, I was more than ready.

15th August 2019. All this hospital stuff I've had to put up with this year has been a bit of a wake-up call. I have spent most of my working life beating the system. "Larking about on the wireless" as my mum once put it. But seeing first-hand how hard hospital staff have to work and how dedicated, caring and cheerful they remain has really brought it home to me that I have never really given anything back. I've had a charmed life "muckin' about and playin' the music". As a patient it's easy to get frustrated when you ask a nursing assistant for something and they promise to come back in two minutes only to leave you high and dry for two hours or even until the next day or in some cases you never see them again. But the hours they put in and the genuine good they do has left me feeling that I have wasted my life. Although it's far too late now to get a "proper job". These people are certainly not in it for the money, it's a true vocation and they should be proud of themselves. Apart, of course from the nurse who nearly killed me in Leighton. But I dare say there's always one bad penny.

27th August 2019. It's a scary step into the unknown tomorrow when I have my very first chemo session. No idea what to expect. I never ever thought this would happen to me, but I suppose everyone says that. I can't help feeling a bit cheated because Lynn and I had such big plans for our retirement. Just goes to show that you should live for today! I now know how my mum was feeling towards the end, she had a load of money saved up but was too ill to enjoy it. It's a bugger and no mistake.

3rd September 2019. Just experienced my first chemo session and for the first two days I felt fine, but then it wiped me out and I have been in bed virtually ever since. It's my second session tomorrow so we'll see what happens. In the meantime, I'm sort of back in the land of the living. Sort of.

9th September 2019. Looking forward to a chemo free week ahead. For those of you who have had to suffer chemo, you'll know that not only is it very scary but also incredibly boring. You go in at nine in the morning to be wired up and you sit there until they finally release you at about five in the afternoon. This bomb disposal stuff they release into your body is so powerful that if they spill so much as a spoonful on the carpet it goes up like an inferno!

Last week I walked in and was asked to choose a seat and before I knew it, there I was, chained up for the day. What I didn't realise was that I had decided to sit right next to the radio … and wouldn't you know it … they had Smooth FM on or as I like to call it Snooze FM. The worlds dullest and most soporific radio station. My Signal Radio colleague, Dave Johnson, once described it as a "comfy beige cardigan" and I know what he meant! For me, it's the very opposite of what radio should be about. I'm sure that when Marconi shot down to the 'patents office' all those years ago to register his new invention, 'Smooth' was the last thing on his mind. I know it's popular and the audience figures are impressive, but popular doesn't make it good.

12th September 2019. For the past few months I've been feeling very sorry for myself, mooching about the house in my scruffs and taking far too many painkillers. This week I decided to pull myself together, halve the painkillers and get out a bit more meeting friends etc. It all seemed to be working fine and I was feeling better than I have for months until I woke up at 4 o'clock this morning with a sky-high temperature and ended up back in hospital. It was a weird feeling, shaking and shivering but in reality, boiling up a storm! One step forward three back. I thought I might have to stay in but they seem to have taken pity on me.

24th September 2019. Back on the boring chemo tomorrow. Now most of the people I speak to tell me that when they had chemo, they were completely out of it, totally knackered, unable to talk, head aches - you name it. But I feel OK. In fact, I feel better than I've done for ages. I'm starting to think there's been a mix up at the lab and that they have accidentally mixed the chemo stuff up with dandelion and birdmuck and that's what I'm being drip fed with. Maybe tomorrow I should ask a few questions.

Had an appointment at the hospital today with the dietician. That's money for old rope if you ask me. The girl was about 14 and she's recommended that I scoff plenty of cream cakes! I think I can manage that. 25th September 2019. Unable to have the chemo yesterday because my temperature was through the roof. Still kept in all day having drips and stuff. Finally got home at 10pm. Just going back now for a full day's MOT. I'm sick to death of needles!

26th September 2019. Well, there's another day of hanging around I'll never get back! They did scans and tests to try and find out why I keep getting infections but can't find anything wrong, which I suppose is good news. I just wish the doctors didn't keep telling me I only have months to live. I INTEND TO BEAT THIS AND DEFY MEDICAL SCIENCE. SO THERE!

27th September 2019. I'm just back from seeing my GP and was able to tell her that just lately I have been feeling much better. I foolishly mentioned that I had even gone back to work one day a week. When she asked me about the work, I felt more than a bit embarrassed. I mean it's hardly work is it? Nowhere near a proper job! 8th October 2019. Had a meeting this morning with the lovely McMillan nurse Lesley in which you're encouraged to open your heart about all the things that are concerning you. Well, it got a bit emotional and I ended up blubbing like a baby which was the last thing I really wanted to do. Very embarrassing.

28th October 2019. Absolutely full of a cold today, spent most of the day in bed. Every time I start to feel poorly, I panic in case I end up back in hospital, but I think the long sleep has made me feel a bit better. I got a letter this morning from those good people at McMillan inviting me to attend a new innovation – 'make up classes' for men suffering with cancer! Lynn thinks it might be a lark but I don't think I'll bother. I have visions of me coming out of there looking like Quentin Crisp.

19th November 2019. Had an appointment at the hospital with the dietician this morning and guess what? After losing two and a half stone in the past few months I have finally put a stone back on. That's possibly the only really good news I've had all year!

CHAPTER 19: "That's All ..." Genesis 1983 (Number 16)

I think we should just about leave it here. Dear reader, you are now up to date with everything that has been happening in my life and, as I have said before, I really have no idea what to expect in the future.

I have been pain free for some time now and have been trying to get on with my life. Lynn and I have been to the pictures a few times. I had not been to the cinema since I took myself off to see 'Fatal Attraction' in 1987 but suddenly, I can't keep away. And what a transformation. These days a trip to the flicks is a bit like visiting a private Gentleman's club. We've also been out for meals and seen a couple of shows. Indeed, I had been feeling so well that Lynn suggested I approach Signal about getting back on the radio. Early on in my illness I received an e-mail from Signal Radio's Chief Executive promising me that if I ever wanted to go back, my show would be waiting for me. To be honest that's the last thing I wanted. I have received good will messages from virtually all the staff at Signal, even people in the offices who I had no idea of their names or what they did. The only people I have never heard from, no e-mail, no text, no phone call, no letter, no nothing have been my two line-managers. The Group Programme Controller, Terry Underhill, and Signal's Head of Programmes, Simon Monk, have never once got in touch to see how I was getting on. This has been scratching away at me like an itch I couldn't reach. I think it's really appalling, so nothing could persuade me to return to Signal.

A former colleague said that he thought Signal had been very good to me over the years, but I think it's probably the other way around. I reckon I've done far more for them than they have ever done for me. For instance, when I took over the breakfast show in 2002 the station's listening figures were so poor that the then owner Kelvin McKenzie was threatening to close the station down. To be fair, he had a point. At the time it would have been easier and cheaper to open the windows and shout. Then there were the songs. "Father Christmas Stole my Girl" was written as a joke, a bit of an amusing filler to play on the breakfast show, but it became so popular that we ended up selling over five thousand copies with all proceeds going to a local good cause. "Standing Together" was my 2006 World Cup song that everybody wanted to buy. In my humble opinion, it's the third greatest football song ever and a lot of people seemed to agree. It raised over £50,000 for charity and entered the charts just above Madonna and Paul Simon despite only being available in one Stoke-on-Trent shop. Something that has never been done before or since!

And ... prior to the cancer irritation, I only ever missed one breakfast show in 15 years due to illness. With Signal out of the running, I made the decision to join another radio station based in Staffordshire and it turned out to be one of the best decisions I have ever made. HitMix Radio has given me a new lease of life and I am loving being back on the radio. Run by a great bloke called Robbie Benson and his lovely wife Jane, HitMix is a breath of fresh air! You very rarely hear the same song twice and it genuinely cares about its listeners. I only wish it was around at the start of my career rather than the end of it. The one regret I have about my life in Radio is never winning a Sony award. The Sony's are the radio equivalent of The Oscars and I honestly believe I deserve at least one. I think some of the programmes I have presented over the years have been funny and ground-breaking. The truth is, if you want to win a Sony you have to have a team working with you all year round. Sadly, I have never had that. One of my best friends who does the breakfast show on a very big station in the Midlands used to get his wife to tape my shows then he would repeat it virtually word for word the following day. He has won three Sony awards, and yes … he is still my mate.

I am glad that I never took my Mum's advice to give up this radio lark and get a proper job. On the whole, I have enjoyed what I do and hope to carry on with it for as long as I possibly can. It has been very rewarding and humbling over the last few months or so to read all the messages of support and good wishes for both myself and Lynn from so many people - friends, colleagues and loyal listeners. In my mind I have just been sitting in a darkened room 'muckin' about and playin' the music' but it seems there are a lot of people out there who enjoy what I do and many who have been listening to me for many, many years. It makes it all worthwhile to know you are there and will be to the end.

Thanks to one and all from the bottom of my heart and I hope you have enjoyed reading about my simple life as much as I have enjoyed telling you about it.

The Last Word from Geoff Lloyd Multi Award winning Radio Presenter & Radio 5 Live Broadcaster. The first rule of radio broadcasting is to talk as if there's only one person listening. I began my career at a local radio station in Stockport, in the prestigious 6am-on-a-Sunday-morning slot. Most weeks, it was difficult to imagine even that single listener. The phone lines were dead, despite (what I believed to be) ground-breaking items such as *Who's On Helium*? and *Name That Bernard!*

As 10am approached, though, the studio switchboard would begin to light up. I quickly - and painfully - discovered this was nothing to do with me, but it was in anticipation of Jumpin' Johnny Owen, who would shortly be, in his own words, 'mucking about and playing the music'. Johnny was the radio station's star player, and also hosted the weekday drivetime show. He'd burst out of the speakers and throw up conversational balls into the air for his listeners to bat back: nuggets of pop culture, music curiosities, long-demolished local nightspots, forgotten footballers, treats from his mental museum of extinct confectionery and fizzy drinks. Every time Johnny took to the airwaves, his audience would jam the phones (and fax machine – this was the early 90s) to see if they could beat his encyclopaedic knowledge of modern trivia. They couldn't, but everyone had a lot of fun trying.

Wonderful as the discussions of *Torchy the Battery Boy* and airings of the *Calamity Jane* soundtrack were, the best bits of Johnny's shows were the anecdotes from his own life. He's an incredibly gifted and funny storyteller, as natural on-air as over a pint in The Pineapple pub next door, albeit with less salty language. You'd be surprised at how little attention is normally paid to what's coming out of the speaker in most radio station offices, but we'd always turn the volume up, listen and laugh as Johnny spun gold from his Lowry painting-meets-*Billy Liar* childhood, his teenage fumbles and romantic rejections, his disco days as a Manchester Tony Manero, and his exploits on the peripheries of show-business.

Radio is transient – once something's been broadcast, it's gone. That fleeting nature is part of the magic of the medium, but sometimes those moments are so good, you want to keep hold of them. That's what this collection of stories is: moments not just from Johnny's life, but from his life on-air. If you've loved listening to his shows, you'll find your favourite stories in these pages (a few so well-worn you'd be able to recite them), alongside many more that he's sharing here for the first time.

I've been lucky enough to eke a living out of radio in the decades since I worked with Johnny, and over those years, I've come to realise that first rule I learned in Stockport is wrong: the best broadcasters don't make you feel like you're the only one listening, they make you feel like you're part of their gang. That's what Johnny Owen does better than anyone.

Johnny's All Time Top 20 Favourite Records.

1. WATERLOO SUNSET - THE KINKS

2 YOU GAVE ME A MOUNTAIN - ELVIS PRESLEY

3 ALL MY LOVING - THE BEATLES

4 THE MORE I SEE YOU - CHRIS MONTEZ

5 AT THE TOP OF THE STAIRS - THE FORMATIONS

6 IN MY LIFE - THE BEATLES

7 MEMORIES - ELVIS PRESLEY

8 BORN TO RUN - BRUCE SPRINGSTEEN

9 FATHER AND SON - CAT STEVENS

10 TOWER OF STRENGTH - FRANKIE VAUGHAN

11 GIRL WHY DO YOU WANNA MAKE ME BLUE - HE TEMPTATIONS

12 AIN'T NO PLEASING YOU - CHAS AND DAVE

13 THINGS WE SAID TODAY - THE BEATLES

14 MY HEARTS SYMPHONY - GARY LEWIS AND THE PLAYBOYS

15 WOMAN - GARY PUCKETT/UNION GAP

16 FOREVER - ROY WOOD

17 IT'S GETTING BETTER - MAMA CASS

19 I'M NOT IN LOVE - 10cc

20 HANDBAGS AND GLADRAGS - CHRIS FARLOWE

Lightning Source UK Ltd.
Milton Keynes UK
UKHW022023051120
372859UK00003B/17

9 781916 258297